HOLIDAY
IDEAS
FOR
YOUTH
GROUPS

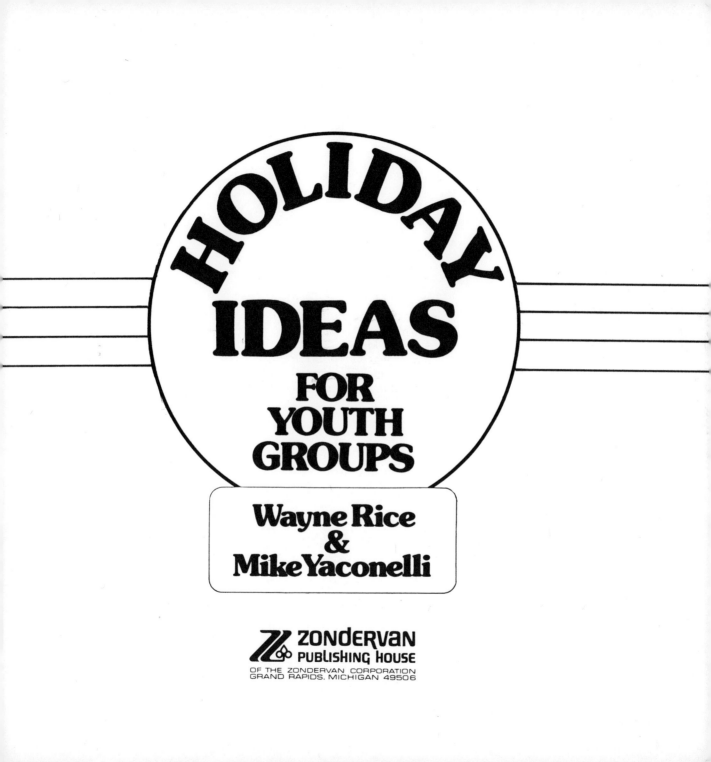

# HOLIDAY
# IDEAS
## FOR
## YOUTH
## GROUPS

**Wayne Rice
&
Mike Yaconelli**

ZONDERVAN
PUBLISHING HOUSE
OF THE ZONDERVAN CORPORATION
GRAND RAPIDS, MICHIGAN 49506

HOLIDAY IDEAS FOR YOUTH GROUPS
Copyright © 1981 by Youth Specialties, Inc.

Zondervan Publishing House, 1415 Lake Drive, S.E., Grand Rapids, Michigan 49506

**Library of Congress Cataloging in Publication Data**

Rice, Wayne.
     Holiday ideas for youth groups.

     1. Entertaining. 2. Games—United States. 3. Youth—United States—Recreation. 4. Holidays—United States. I. Yaconelli, Mike. II. Title.

GV1471.R49          793.2'1          81-13065
ISBN 0-310-34991-5                   AACR2

*Edited by Debra Kool*

The pronouns *he/him* and *she/her* are frequently used generically and interchangeably in this book. ·

*Printed in the United States of America*

84   85   86   87   88 — 10   9   8   7   6   5

# Contents

# Preface

Holidays are special times of the year, and they are made even more so when people get together to enjoy them. This book has been created to make those times of getting together, particularly with young people, as special as possible.

Inside are hundreds of holiday ideas that you can use for parties, socials, special events, youth meetings, special programs, service projects, Sunday school classes, church services—or anytime. Nor are they limited to just one age group. They can be used with children, youth, and adults just as effectively.

We hope you will keep in mind that an idea is only that—an idea. There is no law that says you can't change it, adapt it, or combine it with another. That's called being creative, and we hope that this book will make you very creative indeed.

We would like to thank all the people who initially invented the bulk of this material. Many of the ideas in this book originally appeared in the Youth Specialties IDEAS books, contributed by hundreds of the most creative youth workers in the world, whom we respect and admire very much.

WAYNE RICE
MIKE YACONELLI

# Valentine's Day

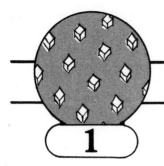

# Valentine's Day

## 1

## Fun and Games

### THE BIG DATE

The following skit works great for Valentine's Day. A teenage couple, Bill and Karen, have just met each other after being introduced by common friends. This is the first date for both. They have just arrived at a local restaurant for a meal.

*Bill:*     *(Embarrassed)* Hi, Karen.

*Karen:*     *(Equally embarrassed)* Hi, Bill.

*Bill:*     *(Still embarrassed)* Hi, Karen.

*Karen:*     *(Still embarrassed)* Hi, Bill.

*Bill:*     Gosh, this is so . . . *(He leaves sentence floating.)*

*Karen:*     Yes, it is so . . . *(She also leaves the sentence floating.)*

*Bill:*     Karen, eh, have you had many dates before?

*Karen:*     The only date I've ever had was on August 13th.

*Bill:*     Oh really, what was that?

*Karen:*     My birthday. *(Karen then drops her comb on the floor.)*

*Bill:*     Oh here! I'll get it. *(As he stoops over, he falls down on the floor.)* I guess I fell for that one, but at least I had a nice trip. *(As Bill stands up, he forgets to pick up the comb.)*

*Karen:*     Oh, Bill, you're so funny! *(Suddenly serious)* But would you mind picking up my comb?

*Bill:*     *(Embarrassed)* Oh yeah, I guess I forgot. *(As Bill squats down, sound effects are heard of his pants ripping. As he reaches behind him to check out what part ripped, he falls backwards from his squatting position over to his back. At that moment a waiter comes to take the order and not seeing Bill, trips over him and falls to the floor.)*

| | |
|---|---|
| *Karen:* | Oh my goodness! |
| *Waiter:* | *(Regaining composure)* What in the world were you doing on the floor sir? Aren't our seats comfortable enough? |
| *Bill:* | Oh no. The seats are just fine. I was just checking to see if the floor was on the level. |
| *Waiter:* | *(Unbelievingly)* I don't know about the floor, but are you on the level? *(Waiter then notices the rip, and seeing the chance for a pun replies . . .)* By the way sir, something *terrible* has happened to your pants. |
| *Bill:* | Yes I know. Isn't that a rip-off? *(Both men stand.)* |
| *Waiter:* | Well, would you like me to do anything? |
| *Bill:* | Yea, how about turning your head when I leave? |
| *Waiter:* | *(Unbelievingly)* Sure thing . . . Hey, I'll be back in a minute to take your order. *(As waiter leaves, Bill sits back down at the table.)* |
| *Karen:* | Bill, I really appreciate your efforts, but my comb is still on the floor. |
| *Bill:* | I'm sorry, Karen, but that waiter crushed my ear when he fell on me. What did you say? |
| *Karen:* | I said my comb is still on the floor. |
| *Bill:* | *(Sheepishly)* Your phone is in the store? |
| *Karen:* | NO! MY COMB IS ON THE FLOOR! |
| *Bill:* | *(Sheepishly)* Oh! I'm sorry. *(Bends down and gets the comb.)* Well, we may as well order, there's no use in waiting around. |
| *Karen:* | I don't mind waiting. Sometimes I even like to wait around. |
| *Bill:* | What? |
| *Karen:* | I said, it gives me a lift sometimes to wait. |
| *Bill:* | Yea. I like weightlifting too. |
| *Karen:* | Oh good-grief. Not to change the subject, but what did you do today? |
| *Bill:* | I got things all straightened out. |
| *Karen:* | What do you mean? |
| *Bill:* | I mean I did my ironing. Aren't you *impressed*? |
| *Karen:* | Not a great deal. I did my laundry today. |
| *Bill:* | I thought I smelled bleach! But I thought it was just your hair. |
| *Karen:* | *(Offended)* Well, I never . . . |
| *Bill:* | Well you ought to, I can't stand the color of your hair. |
| *Karen:* | BILL! You've hurt my feelings! |
| *Bill:* | *(Bashfully)* Oh, I'm sorry. Speaking of laundry, do you know the money changing machines they have in there? |

| Karen: | Well, not personally, but go ahead. |
|---|---|
| Bill: | Well, I wanted to prove how stupid those machines are, so I put a five-dollar bill in one and it still gave me change for a dollar. Just to make sure it was no fluke, I put a ten-dollar bill in the next time and it *still* gave me change for a dollar. I bet you never realized how *stupid* those machines are, have you? |
| Karen: | That doesn't make sense. |
| Bill: | What do you mean? |
| Karen: | I mean you lost thirteen dollars and you are saying the *machines* are stupid. |
| Bill: | Well, I only did it for a change. |
| Karen: | That's what all the money changers are for; a change. |
| Bill: | That makes sense. |
| Waiter: | I don't mean to interrupt, but are you ready to order? |
| Bill: | Huh? |
| Waiter: | Your order? |
| Bill: | What? |
| Waiter: | ORDER, ORDER! |
| Bill: | What are you, a judge? |
| Waiter: | I don't know about that, but whenever I go to play tennis I wind up in a court. |
| Bill: | You ought to get out of that racket. |
| Waiter: | (Looks up and states pleadingly.) Why me? . . . Have you decided what you would like to eat? |
| Bill: | Yes, I'll take the New York Sirloin steak, baked potato, corn, tossed salad with French dressing, and a large Coke. That's all. |
| Karen: | What about me, Bill? |
| Bill: | (Surprised) Aren't you going to buy your own? |
| Karen: | Of course not, it's not proper. |
| Bill: | O.K. O.K. Waiter, she'll have a small Coke. |
| Waiter: | You're not going too far *overboard* are you? |
| Bill: | Don't be silly. We're nowhere near water, much less on a ship. |
| Karen: | You may be right there, but you're *still* all wet. (Karen then throws her glass of water all over Bill and they exit.) |

## BIRDIE ON THE PERCH/ANATOMY SHUFFLE

Here's a good active game for Valentine's parties. Have boy-girl couples get into a two-circle configuration with the boys on the inside and the girls on the outside.

13

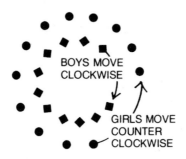

BOYS MOVE
CLOCKWISE

GIRLS MOVE
COUNTER
CLOCKWISE

When the game starts, the boys should begin moving in a clockwise direction and the girls should move in a counter-clockwise direction (or vice versa). On a signal (like when the music stops, or on a whistle), the boys must immediately get down on one knee with their other knee forming a "perch" for the girl. The girl must quickly locate her boy partner and sit on the perch. The last couple to get in position is out of the game, and the game continues until only one winning couple remains.

"Anatomy Shuffle" is played similarly, except that the leader yells out two parts of the body, like "KNEE-ELBOW." The couples must quickly locate each other and touch those two parts of the body together. For the above example, the girl would touch her knee to his elbow, or he would touch his knee to her elbow (either way is okay). The last couple to have those two parts of the body touching is out of the game. You can decide which parts of the body to call out, depending on your crowd. These suggestions are usually fun: NOSE-EAR, NOSE-BELLYBUTTON, CHIN-TOE, ARMPIT-NOSE, EAR-REAR, FINGER-NOSE, NECK-NECK, LIP-LIP.

## COMPATIBILITY TEST

This Valentine's Day game is designed after television's "Newlywed Game," but it is not necessary to use newlyweds. Select two or three couples that have been dating for awhile and have them come to the front. The guys must leave the room, then you should ask the girls a few questions about their boyfriends like Is your boyfriend tight or generous when it comes to spending money on a date? or Is your boyfriend a good or bad driver? The boys can then be brought back into the room and must answer the same questions. If their answers are the same as the girls', they will receive points. If they are wrong, they will get points taken off or will receive a penalty of some kind.

## COURTIN' COMMUNITY

Here's another fun skit that works great for Valentine's Day activities. Characters needed:

Narrator
Father (Mr. Harold Cobb)
Mother (Mrs. Gladys Cobb)

Son (Tobbie)
Courter (Arnold)
Daughter (Carol)

The setting is a living room. Mrs. Cobb is entering the room after talking with their teenage daughter, who is backstage preparing for her big date. Mr. Cobb is seated in the room waiting to continue a chess game with his wife. Their young son is also in the room.

**Act One:** Father, mother, and young son rehash the parents' early years of courtship.

Narrator: A man named Cobb married a girl named Webb. It is assumed that Cobb loved Webb the moment he spider.

Mother: *(Entering the room to continue the chess game)* Carol is upstairs getting ready for her date this evening.

Father: Good. Let's start playing again. *(The chess game is half completed. General discussion goes on as the game continues. Father takes his time before making every chess move.)*

Mother: *(Sentimentally)* When did you first discover that you loved me, darling?

Father: Oh . . . probably when I found myself getting angry every time I heard someone call you an idiot. *(Father laughs and continues to make deliberate chess moves.)*

Mother: Do you really love me, dear?

Father: You know I do.

Mother: Would you die for me?

Father: Of course not, honey. Mine is an undying love! *(Father laughs and continues to make deliberate chess moves.)*

Mother: I like playing this game. This reminds me of when we were dating.

Father: We never played chess in those days, Gladys.

Mother: No, but even then it took you two hours to make a move. *(This time Mother laughs.)*

Father: Son, your mother gets very historical when nights like this come.

Son: You mean hysterical, don't you?

Father: No, I mean historical. She always digs up the past. *(Father chuckles.)* I just was not in any hurry. I had my share of thrills before I met your mother. I remember when I thought I'd met the girl of my dreams–Sheryl. We met at a party and then went out dining and dancing. Afterwards, I asked for her telephone number. She said, "It's in the book." And when I asked her for her last name, she replied, "That's in the book, too." *(Everybody laughs.)*

Son: Dad, how did you meet mom?

Father: Well, it was this way, son. I met your mother through a dating service—her mother.

*(Doorbell rings. Their daughter's young courter is at the door.)*

**Act Two:** Family meets the young courter. (The setting has father answering the door as the courter waits nervously.)

| | |
|---|---|
| *Courter:* | Hello. Is Carol ready? |
| *Father:* | Not yet. Come on in. *(Closing the door)* You must be Arnold. |
| *Courter:* | Yes sir. |
| *Father:* | Well, I'm Mr. Cobb and this is my wife, Gladys. |
| *Courter:* | Hello, Mrs. Cobb. |
| *Mother:* | Hi. Where did you get those beautiful eyes? |
| *Courter:* | *(Shyly)* Th-th-they came with the head. *(Everyone laughs and the tension is broken.)* |
| *Father:* | Arnold, this is our son, Tobbie. *(Going over to the stairway, Father yells.)* Carol, Arnold is here! |
| *Carol:* | Coming! *(She yells from backstage.)* |
| *Father:* | *(Sarcastically)* She'll be right down. You'll probably have time to play a game of chess. |
| | Here, have a seat. What can you tell us about yourself? |
| *Courter:* | Well, there's not much. I play all kinds of sports. I play football. I'm the quarterback. Whenever they toss the coin at the beginning of the game, my coach always calls me over and says, "Go get the quarter back." |
| *Father:* | That's pretty good! What does your father do for a living? |
| *Courter:* | Oh, he's a tax assessor. What do you do? |
| *Father:* | I'm a plumber. |
| *Courter:* | Why did you become that? |
| *Father:* | My wife was always saying she liked a man with a pipe. *(Laughter)* |
| *Mother:* | Harold, quit pestering that boy. |
| *Father:* | Oh, I was just making conversation. It brings back memories of when I was dating, and thinking of marriage. |
| | In fact, it was very difficult for me to get married. I had an enormous problem finding someone who loved me as much as I did. |
| | When I was in my 20's, I went crazy over a girl. For a long time we had a love-hate relationship. I loved her and she hated me. |
| | This was probably due to our religious differences: I was broke, and she worshipped money. |
| | Then I met Gladys. Gladys and I were only half serious about getting married. She was, and I was not. |
| | *(Daughter enters the living room.)* |

**Act Three:** Young couple prepares to leave for the evening. (The setting has Carol entering the living room, expecting compliments.)

| | |
|---|---|
| Carol: | I'm ready. Sorry I took so long. |
| Courter: | Oh, that's okay. |
| Carol: | *(Addresses everyone.)* How do I look? Do you think I'm pretty? *(Spins, showing off her dress.)* |
| Son: | In a way. |
| Carol: | What do you mean? |
| Son: | In a way far off! *(Backs out of the reach of Carol.)* |
| Carol: | Oh you . . . |
| Mother: | You look fine. |
| Courter: | I think you look fine too. And I know you like flowers, so I went out and bought you a package of seeds. *(Hands a package of seeds to Carol; everyone is dismayed. Son breaks silence.)* |
| Son: | Hey Arnold, did you hear about the bee that got mad because somebody took his honey and nectar? |
| Mother: | Oh, you go to your room, Tobbie. *(Pause)* And you better go too, or you'll be late for the movie. |
| Carol: | Bye mom. Bye dad. |
| Courter: | Bye Mr. and Mrs. Cobb. |
| | *(Young couple leaves the house.)* |

**Act Four:** *(Epilogue)* Young couple out of earshot.

| | |
|---|---|
| Mother: | *(Yells to Carol and Arnold.)* Have a good time. Be back early. *(Talks to Father.)* Well, Carol's dates continue to pour in. |
| Father: | You're right there . . . drip by drip. |
| Mother: | Well, I've always said, "there are three kinds of boys: the handsome, the intelligent, and the majority." |

## CUPID

This is a "she loves me, she loves me not" type of Valentine's game. Make a heart-shaped target and fasten it to a guy's back. Give his girlfriend a bow and arrow (with suction cups on arrows). She should stand about twenty feet away and should be given six arrows. The idea is that if she hits the heart on her boyfriend's back, it means she loves him. Every time she misses, the boy should get a pie in the face.

(Note: Bow and arrow should be the toy store variety. You can use toy pistols with suction-cup darts, also.)

THE RIGHT WAY

THE WRONG WAY!

## DEAR HUNT

This is a good outdoor game which works best with larger groups at a camp, or anywhere there is a lot of room to run around and hide. There are two teams: the boys and the girls. The teams do not have to be even. If the guys outnumber the girls two to one, for example, then you can make the scoring work out so that the girls get more points for each score than the boys do.

The object of the game is to accumulate as many points as possible by "kissing" a member of the opposite team and then having your "kiss" validated at one of the three "Cupid Stations" in your team's territory. Both teams must start off in their own territory which is loosely half the field of play (designated beforehand). Once the signal is given to begin, the players should begin chasing members of the opposite team, trying to "kiss" them. This is done by yanking a name tag from their wrist. Each person will have a name tag, which is a 3 x 5 card, hanging from their wrist on a piece of string and a rubber band.

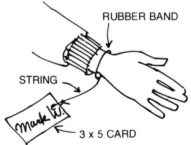

RUBBER BAND

STRING

Mark W.

3 x 5 CARD

Whoever yanks off the tag first has "kissed" the opposing player and that player must then "faint" (fall down) and cease all activity at that moment. After a few moments, the faint player must rise, go to the "Hospital for the Love Sick," and stay there until he or she is able to gain a "new lease on life." This could be for five minutes or so. A new name tag should be made by the resident doctor, and the player will be allowed to re-enter the game.

Meanwhile, the player who makes the successful "kiss" may continue to "play the field," looking for other prospects and trying to keep from getting kissed by an enemy team member. Once a player has made one or more successful kisses, he or she must get his or her captured tags validated if they are to count towards the team's overall points. This can be done by getting to one of three Cupid Stations in their team's area. A Cupid Station is a clearly marked off area where official adult "Cupids" wait to validate tags. Once a player is inside a Cupid Station, he will be safe from attack—but a player can only enter if he has tags that need to be validated. Entering without unvalidated tags causes a player to take a "lover's leap" out of the game completely and sit on the sidelines. Tags can only be validated once. Tags are validated when a cupid signs them on the back, totals up the combined points, and registers these on an official score sheet. Each validated kiss is worth twenty points. If players fail to make it back to a Cupid Station before getting kissed, they will lose the value of any unvalidated tags they hold.

Certain things are not allowed on the field of play: holding of any sort, tripping, kicking, or shoving (in general, anything which would not be allowed on a basketball court). Name tags cannot be concealed or held.

There will be adult "chaperones" watching the play. They have automatic authority to call a halt to any illegal activity and to penalize the offending team fifty points for each violation. Failure to heed a warning or prohibition by a chaperone will result in a 300 point penalty and the removal of the offending person from the game.

Once the signal is given for the game to end, all persons holding or saving unvalidated tags will lose their point value. All cupids should hand in their score sheets and all chaperones their penalty cards. From these the total score minus any penalties will be determined. The team with the most points after penalties wins!

Hospital

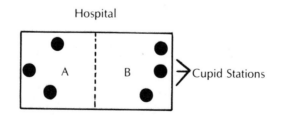

Cupid Stations

### FAMOUS LOVER'S QUIZ

A good simple Valentine's Day game that you can invent yourself is to take a list of famous couples, jumble them up, and make a quiz from the names. The list below is only an example. You can probably think of other couples to add to the list who are

19

more current. But you may also want to include historical and fictional couples as well. Make a few really tough, and kids will have fun trying to figure them all out.

## Match column A with column B:

| Column A | Column B |
|---|---|
| 1. Adam | _____ a. Bathsheba |
| 2. Mark Antony | _____ b. Mary |
| 3. Archie Bunker | _____ c. Juliet |
| 4. Jack | _____ d. Sarah |
| 5. Sir Lancelot | _____ e. Yoko Ono |
| 6. King David | _____ f. Marie Antoinette |
| 7. Rhett Butler | _____ g. Grace Kelly |
| 8. John Kennedy | _____ h. Gracie Allen |
| 9. Henry VIII | _____ i. Queen Elizabeth II |
| 10. Hamlet | _____ j. Eve |
| 11. Romeo | _____ k. Lauren Bacall |
| 12. John Lennon | _____ l. Joanne Woodward |
| 13. Jesus | _____ m. Blondie |
| 14. George Burns | _____ n. Delilah |
| 15. Samson | _____ o. Ophelia |
| 16. Desi Arnaz | _____ p. Jackie Onassis |
| 17. Joseph | _____ q. Dale Evans |
| 18. Humphrey Bogart | _____ r. Jill |
| 19. Louis XVI | _____ s. Cleopatra |
| 20. Roy Rogers | _____ t. Scarlet O'Hara |
| 21. Dagwood | _____ u. Lady Guinevere |
| 22. Paul Newman | _____ v. Anne Boleyn |
| 23. Duke of Edinburgh | _____ w. Dingbat |
| 24. Abraham | _____ x. Lucille Ball |
| 25. Prince Rainier | _____ y. The church |

Answers: 1-j, 2-s, 3-w, 4-r, 5-u, 6-a, 7-t, 8-p, 9-v, 10-o, 11-c, 12-e, 13-y, 14-h, 15-n, 16-x, 17-b, 18-k, 19-f, 20-q, 21-m, 22-l, 23-i, 24-d, 25-g

## FIRST KISS

Here's an "oldie but goodie" that always gets good results. Three guys should be sent out of the room. You can explain to the rest of the group that when each guy comes back in, one at a time, no one is to talk or make any noise. The first word that the guy says is the first word he said after he kissed his girlfriend for the first time.

## FREE KISSES

Before the group comes, put up signs saying; "This way to kissing room," "Test your pucker power," etc. Then on the door of a room, place other signs that say: "Rate your kiss here," "Enter at your own risk," "Prizes awarded to the best kisser," etc. Assign two people, one boy and one girl, to be inside the room. When a person enters the room, have him close the door. Then have the couple bring out a tray of candy kisses and offer the person one. He/she should be told to keep the secret of the game after they leave and maybe even "talk it up a bit." If you think your group will be reluctant to give it a try, clue someone in on the plan to get the action going.

## HEART HUNT

Here's a good game for younger kids at a Valentine's Party. Construction paper hearts of different colors should be hidden around the room. On a signal, the kids must begin hunting for the hearts. After they have found as many as possible, they may begin trading with each other to try and get the colors that they think are most valuable. Players can trade more than one heart of a certain color for one heart of another color. The values will be unknown to the players until the trading is over. The leader can then announce the values and the players can add up their scores. Sample scoring (you can make up your own):

Red Hearts:     10 points each. Five or more, add 50 bonus points.
White Hearts:   25 points each. If you have more than three, subtract 100 from your score.
Blue Hearts:    1 point each. Ten or more, add 100 points to your score.
Yellow Hearts:  200 points. (There might be only one of these.)
Green Hearts:   5 points each. Five or more, add 75 bonus points.

## HEARTS IN HAND

Have the group pair off with one guy and one girl on each team. Place a telephone book or a department store catalog on the floor (any large, thick book will do). Scatter about 50-75 candy hearts all around the book, so that they are within possible reach. As the couple stands on the book, the girl must stoop down, pick up a candy heart, and hand it up to the guy. If they lose their balance and touch the floor, the couple will be disqualified. The couple who picks up the most hearts in sixty seconds wins.

## HIDDEN NAME

Here's a good Valentine's Day mixer that requires a little advance preparation. Each person should be given a name tag to pin to her shirt and a sheet of paper containing Valentine-themed sentences. In each sentence will be hidden the name of someone present at the event. For example:

Please be *gene*rous with your love. (Gene)
I'll be in a *mae*lstrom if you won't be mine. (Mae)
*J'aime* te, mon cher. (Jaime)
Te a*doro thy* lips, love. (Dorothy)

As soon as a person deciphers the name out of the sentence, she must get the signature of the person belonging to that name on her sheet. The names should be spelled correctly, but sometimes a word in a sentence must be misspelled to fit in the more difficult names: "I've been in a ne*beulah*ous state since I met you (Beulah)." The one getting the most signatures receives a prize.

## HOBBY HOAX

Choose three guys in the room who have a hobby (any hobby will do). In front of the rest of the group, explain to them that you are going to ask them questions about their hobby. They must answer but should not give away what their hobby actually is, because later the audience is going to guess what the hobbies of the three boys are. Then send them out of the room (supposedly so that the audience can think up some questions). While they are out, tell the audience that they are to assume that all three boys' hobby is *kissing,* regardless of what their hobbies actually are. Call the boys back in, and ask them questions such as the ones suggested below. Their answers will be hilarious.

1. Who taught you your hobby?
2. How long does it take to do your hobby?
3. In which room do you perform your hobby, or in what place?
4. What sound does your hobby make?
5. Is there any special training involved? If so, what?
6. How old were you when you first learned your hobby?
7. How do you get ready for your hobby?
8. What's the best time of the day to perform your hobby?
9. What do you wear when you are doing your hobby?
10. What sort of special equipment do you need?

## IF YOU LOVE ME

Choose someone in the room to be "It." He must go up to someone in the room and say, "If you love me honey, smile." The person must reply, "I love you honey, but I just can't smile," without smiling or he becomes "It." The person who is "It" may do anything (make faces, etc.) except touch the other person.

## KISS MY NOSE

Select four couples from the audience. The girls should be sent out of the room and the guys must stand behind a sheet which will be hanging vertically and will have small holes in it. The boys should be instructed to poke their noses through the holes in the sheet so that only their noses show on the front side of the sheet. The girls should then be brought back into the room. They will not be allowed to see behind the sheet, but they will be shown the front of the sheet with only the noses exposed. Then the girls must identify their boyfriends' noses by going up to the proper nose and kissing it. After all have done so, the sheet may be lifted, and the girls can see if they have guessed properly.

Then the game should be reversed. The boys must go out, and the girls must stand behind the sheet. However, one of the girls should be replaced with a boy from the audience. The guys should come in and go through the same routine as the girls did, kissing the noses of their girlfriends. Due to the process of elimination, one of them will get a real surprise.

## LOOKING FOR LOVE

Write each name of a famous couple on a slip of paper and mix them up. Then have everyone draw a name and pin it on someone else's back (so that the person they pin it on won't know what the name is). It doesn't matter whether or not boys get male names and vice versa. After everyone has a name pinned to his or her back, each person must find out who she is by asking "yes" or "no" questions of the other people in the room. Each one may only ask one question per person. Questions may include "Am I a man or a woman?" or "Am I someone who really lived or am I a fictional character?" and so on.

When she finally figures out who she is, she must go find her partner (the other half of the couple). If the partner has not yet discovered her identity, then the other person may tell her so that they can pair off. The game should continue until everyone knows who she is and has found her "mate." Some famous couples might include:

Abraham and Sarah
Adam and Eve
Romeo and Juliet
Samson and Delilah
Mickey and Minnie Mouse

Pocahontas and Capt. John Smith
George and Martha Washington
David and Bathsheba
Blondie and Dagwood

## LOVE STORY

Here's a great way to get some laughs at your next Valentine's Banquet or event. Assign each of the following directions to individuals in the group and have each one put down the answer to his direction on paper. After this is done, read the "Love Story" that follows, inserting the answers in the appropriate places.

One good way to do this is to assign each person one of these directions along with the corresponding number. Then have everyone line up front in order. When you get to the appropriate place in the story, point to the corresponding person, who must then read his answer into the story. It's a lot of fun.

1. Name a girl in our group.
2. Name a boy in our group.
3. Describe what you were wearing the last time your mother complained about the way you looked.
4. Think of your favorite activity, but do not write that down; instead, name what you were wearing the last time you did this activity.
5. Write down the most useless advice you have ever received.
6. Write down a sentence from the television commercial you most dislike.
7. Name or describe the place you were when you last received some money.
8. Name or describe the worst kind of transportation.
9. Name or describe what you would least like to be caught doing.
10. Name your favorite food.
11. Name your least liked food.
12. Name or describe the most unusual drink you were ever offered.
13. Name or describe the most unusual thing a person can do on a rainy afternoon.

14. If you were your teacher, what would you have said about the last test paper you handed in? Write this down.
15. Think of the greatest goof you ever made. Write down what you wish you would have said at the time.
16. Name or describe the most annoying habit your brother (or father) has.
17. Name or describe the worst reason a boy could have for breaking up with his girlfriend.

The "Love Story":

Ladies and Gentlemen, we welcome you to another exciting and tearful sequence of the heart-rending soap opera, "As the Stomach Turns." As you remember, during the previous episodes in the fateful life of our heroine, _____1_____ , we saw that her one great desire was to have a date with the hero of her youth, the handsome and debonair, _____2_____ . And now the momentous event has become a reality for our beloved heroine, for he has indeed asked her for a date! The drama begins as we see him arriving at her doorstep wearing _____3_____ . As the doorbell rings, she runs breathlessly to answer it, looking lovely in her _____4_____ . As she shyly greets him, her father looks over his evening paper, takes his pipe from his mouth, and says to the newcomer, _____5_____ . But mother imposes with a tearful _____6_____ . With this, the couple leaves to go to _____7_____ by _____8_____ . Once there, they quickly engage in _____9_____ . Soon, they are hungry, so they go to a nearby restaurant where each orders _____10_____ , topped with _____11_____ , and washed down with _____12_____ . Afterwards, their love deepening as the evening sun spread its amber glow across the horizon, they decide to bring a climax to the date by _____13_____ . As he brings her home again, she lingers on the doorstep, and turning to him with the intense sorrow of parting, speaks these tender words about their time together: _____14_____ . He, holding back the words he wished he were man enough to say, softly whispers, _____15_____ . After the date has ended, she runs upstairs to her room, her heart beating rapidly, and calls her best friend to tell her the exciting evening events by reporting: _____16_____ . Meanwhile, he walks meditatively off into the rising fog. Tune in tomorrow when you will hear him say to his younger brother after returning from the fog, _____17_____ .

## LOVELY CONFUSION

Here's a good Valentine's Day mixer for groups of twenty-five or more. Give everyone the list as printed below. Each person is on her own and the first person to accomplish all ten instructions will be the winner. (They do not have to be accomplished in order, but they must all be done.)

1. Get ten different autographs, first, middle and last names (on the back of this sheet).
2. Unlace someone's shoe, lace it, and tie it again.
3. Find two other people and the three of you form a heart shape lying on the floor.
4. Get a girl to kiss this paper five times and sign her name. _____
5. If you are a girl—have a boy get down on his knee and propose to you. If you are a boy—get down on your knee and propose to any girl. Sign his/her name. _____

6. Eat ten red hots and show your red tongue to someone you do not know well. They sign here. _____

7. Say this poem as loudly as you can.

> How do I love thee? Let me count the ways.
> I love thee to the depth and breadth and height
> My soul can reach. . . .
>
> I love thee to the level of every day's most
>   quiet need. . . .
>      I love thee with the breath,
> Smiles, tears, of all my life!—and, if
>   God choose,
> I shall but love thee better after death.

8. Ask ten people to be your valentine and record your score.

Yes _____ No _____

9. Leap frog over someone five times.

10. You were given a piece of bubble gum at the beginning of the race. Chew it up and blow five bubbles. Find someone who will watch you do it and have her sign here when you finish. _____

## MENDING A BROKEN HEART

Here's a game that is good for getting kids into teams or groups. Make a few large hearts out of red construction paper. There should be one for each team or group that you want to have. Then cut up each heart into as many pieces as you have people in each group. Each heart should be cut up differently.

Each person in the group should be given one piece of a "broken heart." When the game starts, the group must try to find the other members of the group who have pieces of the same heart it does. The first group to successfully get its heart "mended" is the winner.

## MUSICAL VALENTINE

This game is just like musical chairs, only instead of chairs, you use guys who get down on all fours in a circle. The girls should march around the guys, and when the music stops (or a whistle is blown), the girls must sit on the guys' backs. There should be one more girl than there are guys. The girl that doesn't get a guy to sit on is out, and one guy should be removed for the next round. Encourage the girls to "get tough" and really fight for their guy. It's a lot of fun.

## PARENT VALENTINE BANQUET

Rather than the old "Sweetheart Banquet," why not have your young people sponsor a Valentine's Banquet for their parents? The young people should prepare and serve the meal to their parents and then put on a program of skits and special music. Take lots of pictures, have lots of fun, and this may become an annual event.

## SINGING VALENTINE

Here is a fund raiser for your youth group that is effective on Valentine's Day. The group should simply invite people they know to "purchase" a valentine for their "sweetheart" (secretly) on the Sunday before Valentine's Day. You could charge approximately five dollars per valentine. Then on Valentine's Day, the youth group should arrive at the "sweetheart's" house and deliver the surprise singing valentine. The group should all be dressed in red, and several members could be dressed as Cupid. The group may either write fun love songs or sing some well-known ones. After singing (which can be both romantic and silly), the sweetheart should be presented with a "Certificate of Affection" with the secret admirer's name on it. This activity may also involve delivery of flowers and/or candy (for extra cost). The elderly and shut-ins especially appreciate receiving a surprise "singing valentine."

## VALENTINE CANDY CHARADES

Here's a fun game for your next Valentine's Banquet. Get some of those candy "conversation" hearts that have two-to-three-word sayings on them: "I love you," "Slick Chick," "Turtle Dove," etc. One person from the group should pick one of the candies from a bowl, and using the regular rules for charades try to pantomime the message. The person who can correctly guess the saying may eat that piece of candy. You could use teams just like regular charades, or you could do it like the game "Password" with couples who try to communicate to their partners. It is really hilarious to watch the participants try to do phrases like; "Lover Boy," "Kiss Me," and all the other crazy sayings that are on those traditional candies.

## VALENTINE MESSAGES

You should bring three couples to the front of the group and explain that an experiment in "mindreading" is about to take place. You should make a big deal about the implications of ESP, Communications, etc., just to make it interesting. The guys must turn around, backs to the audience, and the girls should be shown a word or sentence like, "Be My Valentine" or "Kiss Me." At a signal the guys must turn around, and the girls should "write" the word on the guys' foreheads with the end of their fingers. The guys should try to guess what the word is by feel, as the girls write. The first guy to figure it out will be the most "perceptive" and will win.

To get a good laugh, do it three or four times, and on the last time put lipstick or soot on the girls' fingers when you give them the word.

# Creative Communication

## LOVE GROUPS

This exercise is a five-session project which could conclude on Valentine's Day. The basic purpose is to let the youth be creative and imaginative about the subject of Christian love through many different activities. The teacher or youth leader should act as a traffic director and organizer and supply very little direct lecture-type teaching.

The basic format of the five sessions will have each youth working in an activity group for the first four sessions. Each of these activity groups will be working on something directly related to the subject of Christian love. During the class period (while the activity groups are working), the leader should stop all the groups for one of a variety of give-and-take sessions which include mini-lectures (3 minutes), discussion, or a short film, all dealing with the subject of love. The fifth session should be devoted to the presentation and action of each of the activity groups' finished products. (For example, the drama group should present their drama, and the "love banners" group should auction off their banners, etc.) Adults or other youth groups can be invited to the fifth session to see and hear the presentations. This could be done on Valentine's Day.

Following are ten sample "love groups":

1. *The Signs of Love Slide Show:* This group will shoot pictures of "signs of love" all around them, have them developed, and create a slide show with narration or music.
2. *Drama:* This group will prepare a play on some facet of Christian love. It can be original, or it can be a well-known Bible story.
3. *The Multiple Listing Group:* This group will come up with lists centered around Christian love. For example, a list of "What love is," or "What love is not," or "Ways to demonstrate love," etc.
4. *The Crossword Puzzle Group:* This group will design one or more crossword puzzles based on the subject of Christian love.
5. *The Poetry Group:* This group will write original poetry about Christian love.
6. *The Cartoons Group:* This group will publish a booklet of Christian love cartoons. They can be original or from other publications.
7. *The Bible Scholar Group:* This group will research the concept of Christian love in the Scriptures using commentaries, other books, etc., and write a report on the findings.
8. *The Love Banner Group:* This group must have some artistic and sewing ability, because they will produce banners on the subject of Christian love.
9. *The Songwriting Group:* This group will compose Christian love songs and perform them. They can be completely original or new words to familiar tunes.
10. *The Love Object Group:* This group will produce love-related art objects to auction off or give away, such as love necklaces, plaques, calligraphy, paintings, or whatever.

Each group should be supplied with the necessary items to complete their work, and the kids should be encouraged to work at home on their projects as well.

## LOVE LISTS

A good Valentine's Day exercise for a group would be to spend some time reading various Scripture texts that deal with the subject of love. Possible choices might be the Cain and Abel story (Genesis 4), the words of Jesus concerning "the least of these" (Matthew 25), or numerous other passages that deal with relationships.

Then divide into small groups and supply each person with pencil and paper. Each person should make four columns on the paper with the following headings: 1. "Intimate," 2. "Close," 3. "Acquaintances," 4. "Distant." Under each column, names of people should be listed according to how "intimate" or "distant" they might be to the person making the list. Maximum for any column should be about five names. The names can be friends and acquaintances at church, school, work, family, or elsewhere.

After each person has listed names in each column, have a time for sharing in the small groups. Each person should explain why certain people were listed under the various column headings and whether or not he is satisfied with his list as it stands. Here he may share feelings, experiences, and school or living situations that contributed to the list choices. In addition, have each person examine his list again and pick out one name from the "acquaintances" or "distant" columns. Have him think specifically about ways to become closer to that person so that he might move up one column. Close with a chance for people in the group to share feelings of closeness or distance that they feel with other members of the group.

## LOVE TEST

Here's a good study based on the "Love Chapter," 1 Corinthians 13. After reading the chapter together, give each person in the group a copy of the test below and ask them to take a personal "love test" to see where they are strong and where they need improvement. The numbers in the left hand column coincide with the fourteen descriptions of love taken from the Scripture and listed below the chart. Follow up with some discussion and try to offer suggestions on how we might improve in each area.

|  | DISMAL FAILURE | SOMETIMES BUT INCONSISTENT | GOOD BUT STILL NEEDS IMPROVEMENT | STRONG AND CONSISTENT |
|---|---|---|---|---|
| 1. |  |  |  |  |
| 2. |  |  |  |  |
| 3. |  |  |  |  |
| 4. |  |  |  |  |
| 5. |  |  |  |  |
| 6. |  |  |  |  |
| 7. |  |  |  |  |
| 8. |  |  |  |  |
| 9. |  |  |  |  |
| 10. |  |  |  |  |
| 11. |  |  |  |  |
| 12. |  |  |  |  |
| 13. |  |  |  |  |
| 14. |  |  |  |  |

1. LOVE IS SLOW TO LOSE PATIENCE
   *I am content to wait without becoming angry when others fall below the expectations I have set for them.*

2. LOVE IS KIND AND CONSTRUCTIVE
   *I am cautious in my judgments toward others and honestly seek to be a healing rather than a hurting presence in my relationships.*

3. LOVE IS NOT POSSESSIVE
   *I don't have to be in control of conversations and other situations in my relationships.*

4. LOVE IS NOT ANXIOUS TO IMPRESS
   *I can relax with who I am and don't have to be the life of the party to feel secure.*

5. LOVE IS NOT ARROGANT AND EGOCENTRIC

   *I don't have an inflated view of my own importance and often find myself concerned about other people's well-being.*

6. LOVE HAS GOOD MANNERS

   *I respect the rights and dignity of others enough not to force thoughtless behavior on them.*

7. LOVE IS NOT SELFISH

   *I'm not always concerned about the rights of me, myself, and I, and find pleasure in the happiness and success of others.*

8. LOVE IS NOT TOUCHY AND RESENTFUL

   *I try to understand others when they hurt me, and I refuse to let hostile feelings generate toward them.*

9. LOVE FINDS NO DELIGHT IN THE SIN AND SHORTCOMINGS OF OTHERS

   *I don't have to reflect on the flaws in other people in order to rest easy with myself.*

10. LOVE REJOICES WHEN RIGHT REIGNS AND TRUTH PREVAILS

    *I get excited when injustices are corrected and am angry enough to pay the price of involvement when someone's rights are violated.*

11. LOVE HAS STAYING POWER UNDER PRESSURE

    *I persevere when the easier route is to run and abandon someone I was once committed to.*

12. LOVE EXTENDS THE BENEFIT OF THE DOUBT

    *I discount the validity of rumors and gossip and continue to believe the best about people until facts prove otherwise.*

13. LOVE SEES WITH EYES OF HOPE

    *I'm captivated by the potential in people and am very much aware that what they are is not what they can be.*

14. LOVE REFUSES TO QUIT

    *When I'm tempted to throw in the towel on a person or cause, I pray for a second wind and hang tough to the end.*

## PARAPHRASING THE LOVE CHAPTER

Valentine's Day would be a good time to allow kids the opportunity to put some of their own thoughts into the "Love Chapter" of the Bible, 1 Corinthians 13. By doing this exercise (it can be done with other portions of Scripture as well), the kids will be forced to think through the meaning and application of the passage. Eliminate key words or phrases from the verses but leave enough in so that the basic idea will still be communicated. Then have the kids fill in the blanks with whatever they think fits best for them. Afterwards compare the paraphrases with the message of the original. The following is an example. Just print it up and pass it out. Let each person read his completed version to the entire group.

*1 Corinthians 13:1–8*

If I have all the ability to talk about _____ , but have no love, then I am nothing but a big mouth. If I had all the power to _____ , but have no love, then my life is a waste of time. If I understand everything about _____ but have no love, then I might as well sit in a gutter. If I give away everything that I have, but have no love, then I _____ . Love is patient, love is kind, love is _____ . Love never _____ .

## TWENTY-FIVE-CENT MATE

This discussion starter deals with the qualities that make people desirable to others as mates or "Valentines." Give a copy of the questionnaire to each person. After everyone has had a chance to complete it, have the group members share their answers and tell why they answered as they did.

Instructions: You may spend 25 cents to "buy" a mate. Select all the qualities you wish from the list below, but do not spend over 25 cents. Put the amount you are spending in the column at the right.

Each of this group costs 6 cents:
A good-looking face          _____
Very popular                 _____
Quite intelligent            _____
A great Christian            _____
Very kind                    _____

Each of these costs 5 cents:
A well-built figure and body _____
A good conversationalist     _____
Tactful and considerate      _____
Happy and good sense of humor _____

Each of this group costs 4 cents:
Large chest or bust          _____
Likes sports                 _____
Attends church—is religious  _____
Honest—doesn't lie or cheat  _____

Each of this group costs 3 cents:
Nicely dressed and well groomed _____
Likes drama, art, and music  _____
Well mannered—comes from nice home _____
Ambitious and hard working   _____

Each of this group costs 2 cents:
The right height             _____
Gets good grades             _____
Likes children               _____
Brave—stands up for rights   _____

Each of this group costs 1 cent:
Choice of color in eyes and hair _____
Owns a car                   _____
Wealthy—or moderately wealthy _____
Sincere and serious          _____

## YOUTH LOVE WEEK

The week surrounding Valentine's Day would be a good time for the youth group to show their love to others in a special kind of way. The group can first compile a list of all the people in the church (or elsewhere) that they would like to express their love and appreciation to and then think of meaningful ways to accomplish this during the week. The list of people can include workers in the church like the pastor, Sunday school teachers, parents, or perhaps senior citizens in the church.

The kids can then brainstorm ideas for something that they can do or give to each person. They might do things like bake cookies, make fruit baskets, take someone out to lunch, visit her, send flowers, babysit for free, send cards, books, singing telegrams, or make special valentines. The possibilities are obviously endless. Something like this can do wonders to build relationships between different age groups in the church and to help the kids to put their love into positive action.

## VALENTINE BALLOONS

In this activity, kids are asked to answer the question, What message would a Christian valentine carry? After discussion, the answers should be written on small pieces of paper and then enclosed in red balloons. The balloons should be filled with helium and released, thus spreading the message of "love" around as the balloons travel. Also on the note should be a request that people respond, so that the kids can see how far their "valentines" traveled.

## VALENTINE'S DAY GRAFFITI

A simple way to get kids involved in sharing their thoughts on the subject of love would be to hang a large sheet of poster board in the shape of a heart on the wall. Written on the heart should be the words, "Love is." Hang it up several weeks in advance and ask the kids to write their definitions all over the heart. Some will be frivolous, but some will be worth discussing.

## VALENTINE FOR A LOST WORLD

To introduce this idea, tell the group that you want them to create a love message that will give hope to a lost world. They should first think through what the message should be, and then each person should construct a "valentine" that would communicate that message. Provide construction paper, scissors, glue, magazines, tape, marking pens, paints and brushes, and so on. Allow the kids to design and complete their valentines. They should be approximately 8½ x 11 inches when folded. Have the group share their valentines with each other. Provide large envelopes for each person, in case she wants to mail her valentine to someone.

## VALENTINE VERSES

Cut out heart-shaped pieces of red construction paper big enough to write on, or get some Valentine's Day cards that have room to write on them. You will need one for each member of your group. On each heart or card, you should write a Bible verse that has something definitive to say about love. Examples: Col. 3:14, 1 John 4:10, John 13:35, 1 Tim. 6:10, Romans 8:35, 1 Cor. 13:4–6, etc.

Then allow each person to take a heart and to share her verse with the entire group. She can also comment on how that verse could be applied in a practical way in her life. Challenge her to keep that verse with her throughout the week and to try to make it a part of her life.

# Easter

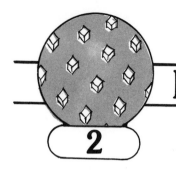

# Easter

## 2

## Fun and Games

### EASTER EGG HOUNDS

This is an Easter egg hunt in which kids pair off—one being the hunter and the other being the "hound dog." The hunters should all gather in a central location, and each hunter should have an Easter basket. On a signal, the hounds must be released and they should take off (on all fours) looking for the eggs. When a hound finds an egg, he may not touch it but instead must begin to howl. When the corresponding hunter hears his hound howling, he must run and gather up the egg. When two or more hounds find the same egg, they should all howl, and the hunter who get there first may keep the egg. Referees should be on hand to make sure that the hunters do not leave the central waiting area until their own hounds call for them. An infraction of the rules will result in the loss of one egg.

### EASTER EGG PASS

This is a relay game in which teams lie on their backs and pass a hard-boiled Easter egg down the line using only their bare feet. The egg should be held between both feet, cupped in the arches of the feet. The first team to get the egg passed all the way down the line wins.

### EASTER EGG ROLLING

For this relay, contestants must roll a hard-boiled Easter egg along an obstacle course with their noses or by pushing it along with a pencil. Eggs do not roll in a straight line very well, making this game a lot of fun to watch. For added fun, decorate some raw eggs and put them into the game without the kids knowing it. It will be a real surprise when the egg breaks.

### EASTER PARADE

This is a funny skit that can be done around Easter to show the latest "fashions" for spring. Set it up like a fashion show with "lovely models" (boys and girls) who try to walk and wiggle like real models. You should also have a good announcer who can describe the various outfits.

Some sample outfits:

1. *Sack Dress:* A dress made of a potato sack, with more paper sacks hung all over it. Maybe even a sack over the model's head.
2. *Dinner Dress:* A dress with menus, napkins, salt and pepper shakers, plates, food, etc. hanging all over it.
3. *Spring-flowered Dress:* Dress with real flowers and metal springs all over it. Purse can be a bucket with fertilizer, tools, etc.
4. *Tea Dress:* Dress with tea bags all over it, and a tea-pot handbag.
5. *Buckskin Jacket:* A jacket with dollar bills pinned to it.
6. *Multi-colored Skirt:* Skirt with crayons and coloring book pictures all over it.
7. *Smoking Jacket:* A jacket with a smoke bomb inside that releases smoke from the sleeves, neck, etc.
8. *Matching Pants:* Pants with matchbooks all over it.
9. *Brushed Denim Jacket:* Denim jacket with paint brushes all over it.
10. *Checkered Skirt:* Skirt with checkers attached.
11. *Tank Top:* Someone with a fish tank over his head.
12. *Pancake Makeup:* Pancakes taped to face.
13. *Lipstick:* Stick held in hand with big lips hanging all over it.
14. *Orange Belt:* Belt with real oranges hanging from it.
15. *Bib Overalls:* Baby bibs sewn to jeans.
16. *Jump Suit:* Model jumps all over the place.
17. *Bell-bottom Pants:* Pants with bells hooked to bottom of legs.
18. *Spaghetti Strap Dress:* Hang wet spaghetti over the shoulders.
19. *Hand Bag:* Outline of a hand drawn on a purse.
20. *Cotton Blouse:* Cotton balls stuck all over a blouse.
21. *Straw Hat:* Drinking straws on a hat.
22. *Choker:* Have someone run on stage behind the model and choke him or her.

With a little creativity, you can probably add others to this list. Pick and choose those you think will go over the best and those you can get props for. If the models really ham it up, it can be a riot.

## EGG AND ARMPIT RELAY

This game requires two teams. Half of the team should line up on each side of the room. The first person must race to the other side with a spoon in his mouth and a hard-boiled Easter egg on it. The player on the other side must take the egg, put it in his armpit, and run back across the room. He must drop the egg from his armpit onto the next person's spoon and so on.

## EGG AND SPOON RELAY

Divide the group into teams and give each player a spoon. The teams should line up, and a dozen raw eggs should be placed on one end of the line. The players must then pass the eggs down the line using only the spoons. They will not be allowed to touch the eggs with their hands, except for the first player who may put the egg on his spoon and start it down the line. The winning team will be the one that gets the most eggs down the line (unbroken) in the fastest time.

## THE GOLDEN EGG

This is an Easter egg hunt for points. You will need to prepare ahead of time a large number of hard-boiled, colored eggs, one of which will be a golden egg. The gold egg can be colored with some gold spray paint, available at hardware stores. The eggs should then be hidden. On a starting signal, the group must hunt for the eggs, and as soon as they have all been found, they should begin trading eggs with each other. Each person should try to accumulate points by trading for the eggs they think have the most value (according to color). At this point in the game, however, they will be strictly guessing, because only you, the leader, will know which colors are worth the most points. After the game is over, you should announce the values of each color, and the kids may then tally up their scores.

Because of the existence of only one golden egg, kids will automatically trade lots of eggs to try and get it from someone else. But you can surprise them by making it worth minus points. At the outset of the game, you should tell the kids that it might be advantageous to try to get various combinations of colors, as they might get "bonus points" for having a certain number of one color, and so on. Encourage them to work out some kind of strategy.

A possible system of points:

| | | |
|---|---|---|
| Each blue egg | = 10 points | 5 of a kind = Add 100 to score |
| Each green egg | = 15 points | All one color = Add 1000 to score |
| Each red egg | = 25 points | One of each color (except gold) = Add 500 |
| Each yellow egg | = 50 points | Most eggs = Add 100 |
| Each purple egg | = 100 points | Least eggs = Add 1000 |
| Gold egg | = Minus 100 points | |

To turn this game into a learning experience, follow it up with a discussion on values, focusing on the idea that it is usually best to know what things are of value and what things are of no value *before*, rather than *after* the fact. The philosopher Kierkegaard once said that life is like a jewelry store in which robbers had entered, but rather than taking anything, they simply switched all the price tags. Things that had great value were cheapened, and things that were of no value appeared to be extremely valuable. Compare this with the world we live in. Ask the kids, "Where do we find the true value of things in life?"; "What are some of the things that the world considers to be of value?"; "What do you consider to be the most important things in life?"

## SQUEAK, BUNNY, SQUEAK

Here's a fun game for smaller groups. Arrange everyone in a circle, seated on chairs. One person should be chosen to be "It" and must stand in the middle of the circle. He or she should be given a pillow and be blindfolded. "It" must then be spun around a few times, the people in the chairs may change seats, and "It" must find a person's lap. He should place the pillow on the lap, sit on it, and say, "Squeak, bunny, squeak." The person who is being sat on should disguise his or her voice and squeak. "It" must then try to guess whose lap he is sitting on. If the guess is correct, the person who has been identified will become the new "It" for the next round. If the guess is incorrect, then the same "It" must try again.

# Creative Communication

## BACK TO THE GARDEN

"Back to the Garden" is a youth program/outing designed to improve the young peoples' basic understanding of the Crucifixion and Resurrection events.

First, develop short scripts (scenarios) based on the following scenes:

A. Preparations for Passover (Matt. 26:17–19)
B. In the Upper Room (John 13:1–14:27)
C. Institution of the Lord's Supper (Matt. 26:26–30)
D. At Gethsemane (Matt. 26:36–46)
E. Jesus Arrested (Matt. 26:47–56, Luke 22:29, John 18:10–11)
F. Trial by Caiaphas (Matt. 26:69–74, Mark 14:66–71, Luke 22:55–59, John 18:15–26)

Select a site which will have a large open room, a meandering path, and several spots along the path where a group can stop and sit. Organize a group of actors (adults and kids) to memorize the scripts and create costumes that reflect the period. Then the people should arrive in groups and begin their walk to the Garden to relive the Easter events.

1. Near the area where people are unloaded, present a scene where the disciples are instructed to set up the Lord's Supper.

2. Take the group to the "upper room" for the portrayal of the Last Supper. At the close of this scene have everyone in the audience also participate in the Lord's Supper.

3. Continue down the path, stopping for the scenes at Gethsemane, Jesus' arrest, and the trial.

4. End the evening by having the group assemble around a large cross (heavy enough so that it takes a number of people to lift it). Give a brief devotional about the cross and then close with the entire group attempting to lift the cross together.

## THE BLESSED BUNNY

The following story can be read to your youth (or adults) as an illustration of how secularized the Easter season has become. Follow up with appropriate discussion questions such as:

1. What is the point of the story?
2. How can Christians combat the intrusion of secular traditions which take away from the true meaning of Easter?
3. What are practical ways the Resurrection of our Lord can be affirmed this Easter?

**The Story:**

It happened the week of March 26. Whoooosh! The spaceship swept low over the Planet Earth and quietly landed in a wooded city park at midnight. Disguised as earthmen three visitors from outer space disembarked and began a week's study of the religious practices of the third planet from the sun.

On April 1 the mysterious spaceship returned and the three hurried on board with their sheaves of notes. Whoooosh! Away they fled, back to Planet Mars.

The next Sunday the three read their report at the meeting of the religious study group who had sponsored their journey. Here is what they said:

"Fellow Martians, it is apparent that a new religion is sweeping the United States of America on Planet Earth. We do not know the name or origin of this religion but we are certain that rabbits are the objects of worship. Do not laugh, brothers. It is true. Earthmen are not as advanced as previously believed. Here out our evidence.

"Religious indoctrination in this belief in the 'Blessed Bunny' begins at birth. Earth babies learn early to positively identify with bunnies. They are dressed in cuddly sleepers which are shaped like bunnies and often have pictures of one or more of the furry animals on the chest. Their beds are painted with happy, playful bunnies and it is not uncommon for an earth baby to sleep with a stuffed bunny. During the early years further identification with bunnies is fostered through picture books and television programs.

"By age four mass religious instruction begins through Saturday morning television programs. Earth children huddle around the TV and watch animated cartoons of bunnies portrayed in many and varied roles. Bugs Bunny is an especially favorite rabbit. His punch line is 'What's up, Doc?' We are not certain of the religious significance of this question. Occasionally a special program is seen in which a rabbit plays a special role. In *Alice in Wonderland,* for example, a crazy rabbit runs around panting, 'I'm late, I'm late, for a very important date.' We are impressed by the results of this mass education. Earth children receive a totally positive image of bunnies and we did not find one child who thought rabbits were anything but good and cuddly and soft. They are 'blessed.'

"Worshipers of the Blessed Bunny observe a sacred week each year in the spring. It is called 'Easter.' Even those who do not adhere to the faith go along with this festive celebration. Businesses promote their wares through the media of bunnies. One sign said, 'Hop on down to your florist.' Another advised, 'Our gas will keep your car hopping.' Bunny-shaped chocolate candy is sold everywhere. Balloons with bunny pictures stenciled on them fly gaily.

"We saw miniature villages populated by stuffed bunnies in several shopping areas. These are apparently worship centers for children. The Blessed Bunny himself appears and sits on a regal throne. Children sit on his knee and hesitatingly talk with him. We felt that the children were awed by this experience and that it has much merit for religious educational purposes. Mar-

41

tians should take note of the fact that earthmen take their religion right into the marketplace where crowds observe the services.

"Song and dance accompany the festive sacred week. We heard many recordings of 'Here Comes Peter Cottontail.' It is also said that a religious dance is practiced by the most zealous adherents. It is called the 'bunny hop.'

"In the teenage years earth children fall away from their religious devotion to the Blessed Bunny. In the late teens and through the thirties, however, male earthlings recover their enthusiasm in a bizarre fashion. The Blessed Bunny himself is no longer the object of their devotion but, rather, some of his helpers who are scantily clad female earthlings called 'Bunnies.' These are distinguished by their large rabbit ears and puff tail. We are not certain, but it appears that the female bunnies are sacred prostitutes. It is said that most young male earthlings are worshipers of the female bunnies. We have no data on that. We did discover that highly secretive temples of worship, called 'Clubs,' have been established in many cities in America. We also discovered that the faithful receive sacred religious literature of this new cult into their homes monthly.

"One sidelight should be mentioned. Although worship of the Blessed Bunny in its several forms is widely tolerated, a small group of heretics take to the fields in the fall of the year to shoot and kill all bunnies they see. They hunt in groups and use vicious animals called 'dogs' to track down the defenseless creatures. The more zealous of these heretics eat the bunnies or make gloves of their soft fur. A growing number of earthmen believe the killing of bunnies should be stopped by the government.

"In conclusion, let us say that we deeply appreciate the opportunity to make this study and to report to you, our fellow members of the religious study group here on Mars. Our studies make us all the more convinced of the validity of our own religious faith. Friends, we need not fear that there is any better faith on Earth.

"For our faith in the Lord Jesus Christ, whom we worship here on Mars, was not challenged in any way by this new religion of the Blessed Bunny which is sweeping Planet Earth. Brother Gregor, who accompanied us, was so moved by the spiritual plight of earthmen that he bore personal witness to his faith in our Lord. A dozen times he initiated dialogue with earthmen, but they would have none of it. Especially did he find resistance to the belief in the Resurrection, that cornerstone of our faith. It is just as St. Paulinus said, 'Jesus is a scandal and offense to many.'

"When Brother Gregor shared the Good News with one earthman, he angrily told him, 'I go to church' and stomped off. We do not know what 'church' is—but, whatever it is, this attender knew nothing of the Living Risen Lord.

"Friends, you know how we have often wondered if the Lord Jesus ever visited any of the other planets in the solar system beside Mars. Well, our study proves one thing. From the earthmen we met and talked with, it is highly unlikely that He ever visited the third planet from the sun."

## EASTER CAROLING

Everyone goes caroling at Christmas, so why not at Easter as well? Decide where you will be going and be sure to inform ahead of time the shut-ins or institutions you plan to sing to. Meet an hour or so early to make sure that everyone knows the songs you will be singing. You might invite the pastor to come and administer communion to the shut-ins and others. Another good idea is to have a group of older folk bring flowers to give to those you sing to.

Be creative with the songs. Vary the songs—use solos, quartets, harmony, unison, and narration. Use familiar songs so that those being sung to can join in. If you carol all afternoon, you may want to have a party, supper, or food-and-fellowship get-together afterwards.

## EASTER COLLAGE

During the pre-Easter season, involve your youth group in a Bible character study of the Crucifixion as recorded in Luke 23 by creating a giant collage of the story. For each of several weeks choose a passage from Luke 23. Have the kids read it. Then choose a key verse(s) which gives some insight into the life, attitude, and feelings of one of the characters. Give each kid a magazine with lots of photos in it and instruct him to find a picture portraying the attitude or feeling of the character as revealed in the passage. Have each person explain his picture to the group. Keep the pictures for each character separate to build a giant horizontal collage, writing out the key verse under the picture cluster. When complete, the collage will "tell" the Easter story. Display the collage during Easter week.

Suggested passages, characters, and key verses are as follows:

| | | |
|---|---|---|
| Luke 23:13–23 | The Crowd | v. 21 |
| Luke 23:13–25 | Pilate | v. 24 |
| Luke 23:26 | Simon | v. 26 |
| Luke 23:27–34 | Jesus | v. 34 |
| Luke 23:35–38 | Mockers | v. 35–37 |
| Luke 23:39 | Criminal 1 | v. 39 |
| Luke 23:40–43 | Criminal 2 | v. 43 |
| Luke 23:46–48 | Centurion | v. 47 |
| Luke 23:50–56 | Joseph | v. 50–53 |

## EASTER CROSSWORD

This is a crossword puzzle that will test a group's knowledge of the events leading up to Easter. It can be printed up and done individually, or it can be done as a group game.

*Instructions (When done as a group game):*

Divide the group into two teams. Teams may elect, or be assigned, to go either "across" or "down." There are an equal number of clues, and it is doubtful that there would be any advantage to being either "across" or "down." There are two, possibly three, rounds in the game. During round one, each team should get a clue (in order) to a word in their section of the puzzle, and will get 100 points for each correct answer. The questions (clues) can be given to individuals on the teams, or to the entire team, whichever you decide. Once the answer is given, it cannot be changed, but wrong answers are not written in the puzzle. Alternate questions between the "across" and "down" teams until you have gone through the entire puzzle one time.

During round two, the missed clues are given again in the same fashion, only this time correct answers are worth 50 points. If there are still empty spaces on the puzzle, then go ahead with round three, awarding 25 points for correct answers this time. Scripture references and Bibles may be provided during this final round.

A good way to conduct the game would be to make a large poster of the puzzle that could be seen by everyone, or make an overhead transparency of it. Do not give the teams the list of clues in advance.

*Clues:*

ACROSS

6. Luke's gospel emphasizes Jesus' humanity by calling Him the "_____ of man."
9. This Jewish leader helped prepare Jesus' body for burial (John 19:39).
11. Jewish high priest at the time of the crucifixion (Matthew 26:3).
12. The Jews also wanted to kill this man because he'd been raised from the dead (John 12:10).
13. The man who carried Christ's cross (Luke 23:26).
14. This ripped from top to bottom upon Jesus' death (Matthew 27:51).
18. High council of Jewish leaders (Mark 15:1, NASB, cross-reference).
19. Natural disaster which occurred when Jesus died (Matthew 27:54).
22. Jesus was His only begotten Son (John 3:16).
23. Wealthy Jewish leader who gave his own tomb to Jesus (Matthew 27:59, 60).
26. The "blood money" paid to Judas was eventually used to purchase this burial place for strangers (Matthew 27:6–10).
27. Woman who annointed Jesus with expensive perfume (John 12:3).
28. He caused Judas to betray Christ (Luke 22:3).
29. The disciple who doubted Christ's resurrection (John 20:24, 25).
31. Jesus said He would rebuild this in three days (Mark 14:58).
35. This Old Testament prophet foretold the sufferings of Christ (Isaiah 53).
37. These were fashioned into a crown for Jesus to wear by Roman soldiers (John 19:5).
38. Roman governor who passed the death sentence on Christ (Mark 15:15).
40. The day of Jesus' resurrection.
42. Jesus died for _____ .
45. Peter was observed in this location when Jesus was taken by the mob (John 18:26).
46. Notorious prisoner released to the Jews by Pilate (Mark 15:7–11).
49. Animal which signaled Peter's denial of Jesus (John 18:27).
50. Jesus performed this service for the disciples in the Upper Room (John 13).
51. Gospel writer who devotes the greatest number of chapters to Jesus' last days (John 12–21).
52. Jesus compared His three days in the tomb to the plight of this Old Testament character (Matthew 12:40).
53. He was chosen by lot to replace Judas among the Twelve (Acts 1:26).
54. This is a symbol of Christ's body, broken for us (1 Corinthians 11:24).
55. The crime which Jesus was accused of by the Jews (Matthew 26:65).

DOWN

1. The cry of the multitudes during Jesus' triumphal entry into Jerusalem (Matthew 21:9).
2. Jesus' purpose in going to the Mount of Olives after the Last Supper was to _____ (Luke 22:40, 41).
3. "This is My _____ which is given for you; this do in remembrance of Me." (Luke 22:19).
4. Roman soldier at the crucifixion who became convicted of Christ's deity (Mark 15:39).
5. In Gethsemane, Jesus prayed to have this taken from Him (Mark 14:36).
7. Signal used by Judas to betray Christ (Matthew 26:49).
8. Occupation of the two men hung with Jesus (Matthew 27:38).
10. Type of branches cast before Jesus as He entered Jerusalem (John 12:13).

11. Christian sacrament which began with the Last Supper.
15. These were cast by soldiers to divide Christ's clothes (Mark 15:24).
16. First person to see the resurrected Christ (Mark 16:9, John 20:11–18).
17. _____ pieces of silver was the price paid to Judas (Matthew 26:15).
20. "The place of a skull" (where Jesus was crucified) (Mark 15:22).
21. Peter cut an ear off this slave of the high priest (John 18:10).
24. Disciple who denied Christ three times (Luke 21:61).
25. Book of the Bible which records Jesus' ascension into heaven (Acts 1:9).
26. The Feast of Unleavened Bread (Mark 14:1).
30. Jesus was made to be this for us, that we might become righteous (2 Corinthians 5:21).
32. Jesus' crucifixion was part of God's _____ of salvation.
33. The resurrected Jesus appeared to two men on the way to this village (Luke 24:13–15).
34. Christ did this for the bread and wine (Luke 22:17, 19).
36. Setting of the Last Supper (Luke 22:12).
39. Animal which was sacrificed at the Feast of Unleavened Bread (Mark 14:12).
41. Roman soldiers dressed Jesus in this garment of scarlet and mocked Him (Matthew 27:28).
42. Young follower of Jesus (later a gospel writer) who ran away without his clothes when he was seized by the mob in the garden (Mark 14:51, 52).
43. The king of Judea who was in Jerusalem at the time of the crucifixion (Luke 23:8–12).
44. Jesus entrusted the care of His mother to this man (John 19:26, 27).
47. Animal which carried Jesus on His entry into Jerusalem (John 12:15).
48. Name for Jesus which means "teacher" or "master" (Mark 14:45).

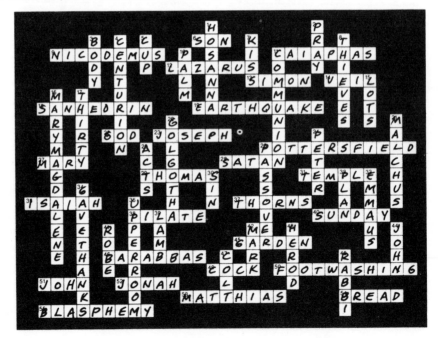

## EASTER I.Q. TEST

Here is a great little quiz that can be used in conjunction with a Bible study on Easter or simply to test a group's knowledge of the Easter story as it is presented in Scripture.

*Instructions:* Place an "x" on the line if you think the answer is biblically correct:

1. The woman (or women) who went to the tomb was (or were):
   _____ a. *Mary Magdalene and the other Mary*
   _____ b. *Mary Magdalene, Mary the mother of James, and Salome*
   _____ c. *Mary Magdalene, Mary the mother of James, Joanna, and others*
   _____ d. *Mary Magdalene*
2. The time of early morning was:
   _____ a. *when the sun had risen*
   _____ b. *while it was still dark*
3. At the tomb was (or were):
   _____ a. *an angel*
   _____ b. *a young man*
   _____ c. *two men*
   _____ d. *two angels*
4. The reaction of the woman (or women) was one of:
   _____ a. *amazement, astonishment*
   _____ b. *fear and trembling*
   _____ c. *great joy*
5. After leaving the tomb, the woman (or women):
   _____ a. *told the disciples*
   _____ b. *said nothing to anyone*
6. The reaction of the disciples at first was that:
   _____ a. *they did not believe the woman (or women); it seemed an idle tale*
   _____ b. *Peter and John went immediately and quickly to the tomb*
7. Jesus first appeared to the disciples:
   _____ a. *in Galilee, on a mountain*
   _____ b. *in an upper room in Jerusalem*
8. Jesus seemingly last appeared to the disciples:
   _____ a. *on a mountain in Galilee*
   _____ b. *on a mountain in Bethany (or just outside Bethany)*
   _____ c. *by the Sea of Tiberias*
9. The gift of the Holy Spirit was given to the disciples:
   _____ a. *before Jesus ascended; in the Upper Room He breathed on them*
   _____ b. *after Jesus ascended, on the Day of Pentecost*
10. We have many details about the crucifixion and death of Jesus. Which Gospel writer gives the most details about the actual resurrection of Jesus from the grave? Which one best describes what happened when Jesus rose from the dead?
    _____ a. *Matthew*
    _____ b. *Mark*
    _____ c. *Luke*
    _____ d. *John*

*The answers are found in Matthew 28, Mark 16, Luke 24, John 20–21, and Acts 1. In questions 1 through 9, all of the choices are correct, and in question 10, none are correct, since none of the Gospels describe the actual resurrection of Christ; only what happened afterward. Obviously this quiz can open up some good discussion on the differences between the four Gospel accounts and how they can be reconciled to each other.*

## EASTER EGG HUNT FOR MEANING

Give each student a giant plastic egg (from L'eggs—the eggs with ladies' hose in them) and ask her to fill the egg with something that to her represents or symbolizes the true Easter message. Have her bring this back on Easter Sunday and exchange it with another's as an Easter gift. As the young people open them, allow each to share why she thinks the person chose that particular symbol of Easter. The results can be very meaningful.

## EASTER ON THE NETWORK NEWS

The following is an outline for a youth sunrise service or Easter program that can be conducted by the youth for the entire church body. Assign the character parts to various members of the youth group. The characters should then study the scene(s) they are to participate in, study the appropriate Scripture, and then work out the necessary dialogue, based on the facts in the Scripture. It is best to rehearse the entire service a few times before its presentation so that it can be refined during the rehearsal process. A songleader will be needed to involve the congregation in singing between the "newscasts." Some of the music, however, can be performed as solos, duets, or instrumentals.

Props do not have to be elaborate. People may use their imaginations. The dialogue is the most important part. You will want to set up a table and chair situation for the "anchorman," similar to a news broadcast on television. Since the idea is to re-create the Easter story as a current event, contemporary dress may be worn by everyone involved. The reporters who are "on-the-scene" may appear in various places around the room or platform. Since the anchorman sets each scene, props are not necessary, but your own creativity and resources can dictate this.

The service may be introduced with remarks similar to these: "This morning's commemoration of this historical event is not one that fits with the usual sunrise service. But we trust that it will be used by God's Spirit to help you celebrate this joyous event. What we celebrate today happened many years ago . . . but what if these events had taken place today? What if God had chosen to reveal Himself, in Christ, to our generation? How might these events have been reported through the news media? That is the setting for this service."

*Scene Synopsis:*

1. *T.V. Newsroom and Garden of Gethsemane:* The anchorman is giving the evening news on Thursday evening. Among other news items, he reports that . . . "Jesus Christ has just been arrested by a Roman battalion. For a report we go to the Garden of Gethsemane." There the reporter on the scene pieces together the story of the betrayal and arrest of Christ, which has just taken place (Matthew 26:47–57). He reports back

to the anchorman. (Suggested songs: *Go to Dark Gethsemane*, *'Tis Midnight* and on *Olive's Brow*)

2. *T.V. Newsroom and Trial "Courtyard": (Late Thursday night)* The anchorman breaks in with a late-breaking news development on the trial of Christ. "For a report we go to the High Priest's chambers." Reporter standing in the courtyard gives a report on the trial (Matthew 26:59–68). Reporter then spots Peter and interviews him (Matthew 26:69–75). He reports back to the anchorman with the trial still in progress. (Suggested song: *Bold Peter Denied His Lord*)

3. *T.V. Newsroom and Governor Pilate's Courtyard: (Friday morning)* The anchorman reports that the trial is over. Jesus has been condemned to die on the cross, and they are leading Him up the hill to Golgotha now. "For a report, we go to Governor Pilate where we have a reporter standing by." The reporter interviews Pilate concerning the trial, particularly his feelings (Matthew 27:11–26). After interviewing Pilate the reporter spots Barabbas, the criminal released in place of Christ. He interviews Barabbas (Matthew 27:15–21). Then he reports back to the anchorman. The anchorman gives an update on Judas, who betrayed Christ (Matthew 27:3–5). (Suggested song: *The Old Rugged Cross*)

4. *T.V. Newsroom and the Crucifixion Site: (Friday afternoon)* The anchorman reports that Christ is on the cross. He reports and comments on some of the strange events associated with the crucifixion (Matthew 27:45–53). "For a report on the crucifixion, we go to Golgotha." The reporter gives a brief account of what happened (Matthew 27:27–50). Then he interviews the centurion (27:54) and Mary Magdalene (27:55–56). (A little more imagination is needed for these two interviews because of little scriptural information.)

5. *T.V. Newsroom and Burial Site: (Saturday morning)* The anchorman reports that Christ's body has been taken down from the cross, bound, and placed in the tomb of Joseph of Arimathea (Matthew 27:57–60). "For a report, we go to the tomb site." Reporter interviews some soldiers who are busy at the entrance of the tomb (Matthew 27:62–66). (Suggested song: *Christ Arose*)

6. *T.V. Newsroom and Burial Site: (Sunday morning)* The anchorman reports a rumor that the tomb in which Christ was laid is empty. "For an accurate report we go to the tomb site where a reporter is standing by." The reporter sums up what seems to be happening. Then he speaks with Mary, Mary Magdalene, Peter, and John, who are standing in a group wondering what happened to the body of Christ (Matthew 28:1–7, John 20:1–10). He also speaks with the guards, huddled in another group (Matthew 27:4, 11–15). He reports back to the anchorman. As the anchorman is summarizing, another reporter cuts in with a report of two men who have seen and talked with Christ (Luke 24:13–35). Almost immediately, another reporter cuts in with a report from Mary Magdalene, who has seen and talked with Christ (John 20:11–18). (Suggested song: *Christ the Lord Is Risen Today*)

7. Final commentary on the weekend's events by the anchorman. (Suggested song: *Alleluia*)

8. Closing comments and prayer by the leader.

## EASTER SLIDES

This is a great way to teach the Easter story (could work for any Bible story), have good fun and fellowship, and have a permanent pictorial and audio record of your youth group.

Have the youth group create a 35 mm slide presentation of the Easter story. The youth group itself should pose for the shots, scout out the locations, find the props, and make the costumes. Write a script for the slides and record it to play along with the slides. Make sure you make a few extra slides to put credits on, so that this can be used for many years and people will remember who posed for the pictures.

Give yourselves plenty of time so if a needed slide doesn't work out, you can take it over. The slide presentation can be made to the entire church, shut-ins, and many other groups.

## THE EXECUTION

The following short play is good for use as a discussion starter or as a statement on the meaning of the Crucifixion. It requires two characters who have speaking parts (Calvinicus and Georgius) and any number of others who carry out the action as described in the column "Visual" below. Calvinicus and Georgius carry on their conversation totally oblivious to what is going on behind them.

| VISUAL | AUDIO |
|---|---|
| Camera (or spotlight) on men eating lunch. | *Calvinicus:* Hi, George, What's new?<br>*Georgius:* What d'ya mean? Nothing ever happens around here. Looks like another hot one. Nice day for camels, eh?<br>C: *(Chuckles)* Yeah, pass me an olive, will ya?<br>G: Here you are, ya beggar. Why don't you get yourself a bowl and sit at the Jerusalem gate?<br>C: Lay off, OK? It's been rough enough today out there in the fields. Look at these fingernails! |
| People start walking across behind the workmen. | G: Yeah, I know. The ground is so hard. Almost broke the yoke right off my ox.<br>C: What's going on anyway? What's all this commotion about?<br>G: Oh, just another execution. You know, one of those weird "prophets." Claim they got the answer to all the world's problems. Bein' executed along with two other criminals.<br>C: Oh. He's the guy. Yeah, I heard about him. They say he's God or something. Some people say he did some kind of hocus pocus on some sick people.<br>G: Yeah. These "prophets" are all the same. They supposedly fix a few legs and eyes and everyone goes ga-ga. Course, he's also charged with creating a disturbance, inciting a riot, and contempt of court. |

A small cross is
carried in and set to
one side.

They never learn. If he really wants a following, he's
gotta explain how come his God is so good at fixing
legs and so bad at gettin' him outta jail. Uh . . . look
. . . I gotta get back to the house and start preparing
for the feast tonight.

C: You know George, just the other day I was telling the
wife what a mess the world is in. On one hand you
got those radical Zealots and Essenes walking
around with the short hair and stuff, and on the other
hand you got those phony loudmouthed Pharisees
running around, blowing trumpets and prayin' in
your ear. What are things coming to anyway?

G: I don't know, man. Why don't you ask Caesar?

C: I know this sounds weird, George, but sometimes I
think if there is a God, I wish he'd do something
radical about what's going on down here. I mean, you
know, he could always come down here and zap a
few Romans. Then maybe something would happen.

A second small
cross is brought in
and set to the other
side.

G: It'd be great if anything would happen around here!
Every day . . . out to the fields . . . plow, plow, plow
. . . grab a lunch . . . back to work . . . crunch the
grain . . . same old grind. What kind of life is that?

C: It sure would be great if we could all go back to the
good old days of sheepherding like the Waltonbergs.

G: Are you kidding? I wouldn't go back to sheep for
nothin'. Progress, man, progress. Oh sure, it gets a
little dusty in town with all the traffic, but this is
where the action is. Of course, all this activity has
made my wife nag a little more (if that's possible).

C: I don't know, man. Seems like I just wake up, turn off
my rooster, go to work, go home, blow out the lamp,
go to bed. I wish there was something more. I'm
beginning to wonder about this religious stuff. I mean,
if there is such a thing as God, why doesn't he just
come down and say, "Hi, folks. I'm God. How'd you
like to see a few Romans made into pizza?"

A third large cross is
slowly brought in.

G: You ought to know by now, Cal baby, religion is all a
bunch of myths and stuff. Well, see you around.

C: OK, George, see you later.

G: (Sarcastically) Heah. By the way, Cal, if you bump
into some guy that says, "Hi, I'm God," let me know
. . . I'd like to meet him.

## MAUNDY THURSDAY EXPERIENCE

This is an excellent way to help make Easter Week more meaningful for your young
people. Have the kids meet on Maundy Thursday (the Thursday prior to Easter) and
participate in the following events:

1. Begin with supper in small groups in various homes. Prepare a discussion guide about what happened at the Last Supper. Have one of the kids lead the discussion after the meal, remaining around the table with all the left-over food and dirty dishes on the table.
2. Meet at the church (or elsewhere) with the entire group and have a Communion service, with all the members of the church, if possible.
3. Take a short trip to "Gethsemane." This can be a nice, isolated park with trees, bushes, hills, etc. Attempt to experience in some way the feelings and thoughts that Jesus must have had at Gethsemane. Sit together in a close group and have someone relate the story of Gethsemane from the Bible.
4. Point out that, just as Jesus, we have our "gethsemanes" too. Have a few in the group share a time in their lives when they felt something of what Christ must have felt. This can be very impressive.
5. Close by joining hands in a large circle and singing Easter songs together.

## SEDER

The Seder is a meal of the Passover celebration that recalls the liberation of the Hebrews from slavery in Egypt. Most libraries have a book of Jewish festivals with a complete explanation of the meal and the symbolic foods that are a part of the ceremony.

The Seder is an excellent way to help your youth group tie together our Judaic and Christian heritages. It is probably the meal that the disciples and Jesus celebrated in the Upper Room the night of Jesus' arrest. This meal should be prepared and eaten on Maundy Thursday. You can close in the Christian tradition with Communion.

## THEOPHILUS TAKES A STAND

This is a play that is centered around evidences for the resurrection of Jesus Christ. The best way to use it for a youth group meeting is to have the two actors stop after each argument presented by Antipas, allowing the group to discuss possible answers to the argument before Theophilus gives his answer.

*Characters Needed:*

Theophilus
Antipas
Announcer (just for the introduction)

*Announcer:* Let us assume that Theophilus (who can be found in the Bible in the first four verses of the Book of Luke) has very recently surrendered his life to Jesus Christ, and the word of his conversion is rapidly spreading. His conversion has us also assume that his decision has resulted in dismissal from his governmental position, but every endeavor is being made to persuade him to renounce his new belief. The present scene opens with Antipas and Theophilus in the midst of conversation. Antipas is extremely upset and is resorting to every rational or irrational argument he can to get Theophilus to change his position.

| | |
|---|---|
| *Antipas:* | Theophilus! Theophilus! Now I know why your name is Theophilus! |
| *Theophilus:* | You do? |
| *Antipas:* | Yeah. Because you have done *Theophilus* thing that you could have done to us, Theophilus! That's why! |
| *Theophilus:* | But sir . . . |
| *Antipas:* | How could you do it? How could you? Do you realize how this has already spread? Don't you know what people are saying? How you've degraded the Emperor and all that we stand for? Theophilus, how do you explain yourself? |
| *Theophilus:* | Antipas, I think you know me well enough to . . . *(Antipas interrupts)* |
| *Antipas:* | I thought I knew you, but after this mad change—this radical—fanatical—O, Theophilus, Theophilus . . . What has happened to you? |
| *Theophilus:* | Antipas, I'd like to share it with you if you'll just . . . *(Antipas interrupts)* |
| *Antipas:* | Share with me! Ha! What you probably mean is that you'd like to convert me too! Theophilus, don't you see that if you want to be religious no one would be opposed, not even the Emperor, but making a public spectacle of yourself—going to such ridiculous extremes—how could you do it? O, Theophilus, Theophilus! *(After a brief pause)* How did it all start? |
| *Theophilus:* | Antipas, it seems to me that my years of service to the Emperor, which have been marked by unaltered allegiance and absolute loyalty, should be sufficient to persuade you that I would not quickly follow after some fly-by-night leader of a false religion. Indeed, it should prove that I would not follow after *any* leader, false or true, without a *great deal* of thought and earnest consideration of its effect on the nation, the Emperor, my family—and myself, if you please. Antipas, for the past six months I have been in correspondence with a man who has had the privilege of interviewing people who were eye witnesses to miracles. And besides, when death did follow—and certainly it soon would have—why didn't someone produce His body? |
| *Antipas:* | All right, all right, let's assume He died. |
| *Theophilus:* | No, Antipas, let's not assume it. He did die! |
| *Antipas:* | All right, all right, so He died, but what actual proof have we that He rose from the dead? |
| *Theophilus:* | Could there be any better proof than an empty tomb? |
| *Antipas:* | That doesn't prove His resurrection. How do we know someone didn't remove His body from the tomb? |
| *Theophilus:* | Who, for example? |
| *Antipas:* | Why—either the Roman or Jewish officials might have moved it. *(Take time for the group to answer this postulation.)* |
| *Theophilus:* | On the contrary, Antipas, the Jewish officials made a request to Pilate to have someone guard the tomb so that the body would not be stolen, but no such request to change it from one place to another was made. However, if either the Jewish or Roman officials had removed the body they surely would have |

known the final resting place; and when the disciples began preaching the resurrection, the High Priest or Pilate or some other official would only have to have spoken out, informing all concerned that they had removed the body to another burial place; thus destroying the possibility of a physical resurrection. And as a last word to the argument, they could simply have produced a body and this would have removed all doubt.

Antipas:          But Theophilus, was Jesus not buried in a tomb owned by Joseph of Arimathea?

Theophilus: Yes.

Antipas:          Is it not reasonable to assume that Joseph had this tomb for his own use rather than to bury someone else in?

Theophilus: Yes, this is quite a reasonable assumption.

Antipas:          And wasn't his tomb rather close to the scene of the crucifixion?

Theophilus: Yes, Antipas, but what are you getting at?

Antipas:          Just this: With all these things being true, it seems quite likely that in the first place Joseph merely planned that Jesus' body be placed in his tomb temporarily, and that at his earliest convenience he would move it to a more suitable resting place.

Theophilus: You will recall, Antipas, that the tomb was found to be empty by a group of women before dawn, which means that Joseph would have to have started work at a rather early hour. It would seem very strange that a respected leader of the people would choose such an odd hour to perform a perfectly legitimate act. In fact, since we are not told that these two groups were aware of each others' presence at the tomb, we must of necessity assume that Joseph and his party began their work in the dark of the night which would necessitate lamps or torches. They would have had to work under maximum difficulty, picking their way through the unlighted regions beyond the city wall, carrying a heavy body probably for some considerable distance, and depositing it into another grave. Then too, we must assume that they went to the trouble of removing all the grave-clothes, leaving them in the tomb and then conveying the naked body to its destination. We also have to consider that they either forgot to close the door of the tomb or did not wish to spend the time doing so. Antipas, this all seems rather unlikely.

Antipas:          Not necessarily so, Theophilus. I grant you that dawn would have been a more ideal time to begin such an operation, but Joseph may well have feared that a task requiring at least two hours for its completion would draw a large and dangerous crowd if undertaken after sunrise. His thinking being such, it seems quite reasonable that in his desire to make the most of the time he left the tomb open and the stone rolled to the side.

Theophilus: This is plausible, Antipas, but hardly probable. As you well know, the priests were very angry with Joseph and he was summoned before the council. You will recall too, that Joseph as a member of the Sanhedrin council did not consent to the death of Jesus as did the others. For he was a secret disciple. But now that Jesus had died the death He died, Joseph seemed compelled to make his sentiments known by offering his own tomb for an honorable burial for Jesus. It seems to me that for one in Joseph's position, having made at long last the sacrifice he had hesitated to make during the Lord's living ministry, the thought that the revered leader and martyr rested in his tomb would have been an imperishable consolation—the one hallowed recollection which would brighten the sad memories of his declining days. Would he have incurred the penalties inseparable from this action—the contempt of his old associates, the deep hostility of the priesthood, the disgrace of declaring himself a follower of the discredited and crucified Prophet—and have been willing within 36 hours to part with the consolation he had found in making a stand for Christ? I doubt it Antipas. Psychology is overwhelmingly against it.

Antipas: But, Theophilus, you must recall that in such times of stress, tension, and grief one does not always react in a logical manner.

Theophilus: This is very true, Antipas. But if Joseph removed Jesus' body to a new tomb these facts would have been accessible to the priests, not to mention the number of men who would have been necessary in helping to move Him. So when in approximately seven weeks the disciples were back in Jerusalem, declaring with the utmost certainty that Jesus had risen from the dead, why would not the officials simply tell the truth and produce the body? *(Pause while Antipas thinks.)*

Antipas: Perhaps Joseph didn't remove the body . . . Theophilus, I hardly know what to say—obviously I don't share your sentiments, but—but, it seems clear that you are convinced that what you are saying is true . . .

Theophilus: Let's put it this way, Antipas, I have finally come to experience what my name actually means—"lover of God." It's no longer simply a title or a name, but I have come to know Him personally, and my love for Him has begun to grow as does a child's for his father.

## THE TOMB REVISITED

This is a modern version of the Easter story. It is not very appropriate for a solemn morning service but is great as a creative way to introduce a story everyone seems overly familiar with. It contains good discussion possibilities.

*Characters Needed:*

Guards (Louie, Bernie, Marvin, Norman)
Chief Priests (Caiaphas, Annas)

The setting has four guards sleeping in front of the tomb of Jesus. They are to snore and awaken without paying any attention to the tomb.

Louie: *(Wakes up, rubs eyes, yawns, and stretches.)* Man is it cold out here—I better build a fire. *(Begins to rub two sticks, puts wood and leaves together, blows into it, etc.)*

Bernie: Hey, wat'cha doing Louie?

Louie: Oh, just putting my Boy Scout training to use.

| | |
|---|---|
| Bernie: | Forgot the matches again, eh? *(Gets up and goes over to a knapsack and finds a box of matches.)* Here ya go. *(Throws matches to Louie.)* |
| Marvin: | *(Awakening from sleep)* Hey what's going on with all the noise? |
| Louie: | *(Testily)* I'm trying to get a fire going for breakfast. |
| Marvin: | Never mind for me—I've got mine already to go. *(Shows a box of cereal and begins to prepare his own breakfast.)* |
| Norman: | *(Who has by this time also awakened–sniffs in the air as if something is burning.)* Hey, what's burning? |
| Louie: | Probably wood. |
| Norman: | *(Walking toward fire)* No, no. It smells like something rotten is burning. *(Pause)* |
| Bernie: | Oh, it's just your imagination. |
| Marvin: | No—I smell something now too. |
| Louie: | What's that in the fire there? *(Pokes a stick in the "fire" and pulls out a burned shoe.)* |
| Norman: | Those are my new Adidas you've been using for kindling wood you idiot. Why I ought to strangle you with my bare . . .*(This last line is said while chasing Louie around the fire. Louis falls at Norman's knees, wraps his arms around him, and begs for mercy.)* |
| Louie: | Please, Norman—have mercy on me. |
| Bernie & Marvin: | Yeah Norman, give him a break. *(Just then Norman notices the empty tomb. His eyes bug out and he says:)* |
| Norman: | Look! The tomb! It's empty! |
| Everyone: | We're in big trouble. |
| Marvin: | We are all gonna get fired. |
| Louie: | *(Crying)* I'm going to lose my pension—and I only had three more years to go until retirement. |
| Bernie: | Don't feel bad? I've got a house to pay for and a son attending Jerusalem State Medical School. |
| Norman: | What are you guys talking about. It's not our fault that the tomb is empty. Jesus must have really come back from the dead—just as He predicted. |
| Louie: | What makes you say that, Norman? |
| Norman: | Well, that rock. It's moved. Who do you think moved it—the tooth fairy? |
| Marvin: | *(Glaring at Bernie)* I'm sure we wouldn't have slept through an earthquake. |
| Bernie: | Well don't look at me—I don't know where Jesus is. |

| | |
|---|---|
| Louie: | Well if it's not our fault that He's gone, let's get down to headquarters and tell the chief priests to put out an APB. |
| Everyone: | Right! *(Pick up sleeping bags, put out fire, etc. as curtain closes.)* |

## SCENE II

The setting is a room with a desk and chairs, depicting the place of the chief priests.

| | |
|---|---|
| Caiaphas: | *(Excitedly)* What are you guys doing here? You're supposed to be at the tomb! |
| Louie: | *(Nonchalantly)* There's nothing there to guard. Jesus is gone. |
| Annas: | *(Very excitedly)* Gone! Where did He go? |
| Marvin: | Norman thinks that Jesus has risen from the dead—just like He predicted He would. |
| Annas: | You nincompoops! We can't have people believing Jesus came back from the dead. Think what it will do to our religion and more importantly—all of our jobs! Why, who is going to give to the Temple if they think there is a risen Savior? |
| Bernie: | Well, what do you want us to do? |
| Caiaphas: | Let us think about it for a minute. *(Caiaphas and Annas huddle for a few moments.)* |
| From the middle of the huddle: | That's a good idea. |
| Caiaphas: | *(Coming back to the guards)* Look. Who else knows about Jesus rising from the dead? |
| All the guards: | Nobody. |
| Caiaphas: | *(Rubbing his hands together)* Alright, this is what we are going to say to the press. Quote: "We do not know the whereabouts of Jesus of Nazareth's body because while the guards were sleeping, His disciples stole Him away." |
| Norman: | That's no good. If we were sleeping, how would we know His disciples stole the body. |
| Annas: | *(Testily)* Look, Norman, we are doing this for you as well as ourselves. This statement will not only save your job but will also make you rich. |
| Norman: | *(Sarcastically)* How? |
| Annas: | *(Pulls out a wad of money.)* This money is for you—if you can keep our little secret. Do I have any takers, boys? |
| Bernie: | *(Greedily stuffs money in pockets.)* I've got a boy in medical school. |
| Louie: | I need a little extra for my retirement. *(Stuffing money into his pockets)* |
| Marvin: | Everybody likes money. |

Norman: (Firmly) Money never brought a man back from the dead though. (Exits right, leaving the others standing in the room with dumb looks on their faces.)

## THIRTY PIECES OF SILVER

At Easter time, an effective way to receive a special offering from your youth for a worthwhile project would be to have everyone bring a plastic sandwich bag with thirty pieces of silver in it. Any denomination of coin is acceptable, as long as it is silver.

# Halloween

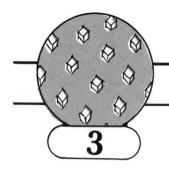

# Halloween

## 3

Fun and Games

### ABDUL THE MAGNIFICENT

This is a mind-reading stunt which, when done right, is downright spooky. Give each person a slip of paper and ask him to write a short sentence on it. The slips should then be folded, collected, and "Abdul" (who can be dressed appropriately) should proceed to perform the task of reading the sentences to the group without opening the papers.

How is it done? Abdul also puts one slip of paper in the box along with the others, only he puts some kind of identifying mark on his. When the reading starts, he picks one of the slips from the box, rubs it on his forehead without opening it, and offers any sentence as a guess as to what is on the paper. He then looks at the paper, and to his dismay he is wrong, but that will soon be forgotten. He could blame it on the fact that the "spirits" weren't quite right yet, but that the next one should be better. It's important not to dwell on this mistake. Just get on with the next paper. It's also important not to reveal what was actually on the paper guessed incorrectly. Just get rid of it and go on. Another slip of paper is held to the forehead, and Abdul then repeats the sentence which was actually on the previous paper. After rubbing his forehead, he opens this second slip of paper, confirms that he is correct, and asks the person who wrote that sentence to identify it. Everyone should be impressed. Another paper is drawn, and again Abdul repeats the sentence that was on the previously opened slip. Each time he opens up a slip of paper to see if he is "correct," he is actually learning the next sentence. The important thing is to stay one slip ahead. When he comes to his own slip, which has been held until last, he repeats the sentence on the previous slip, and that takes care of all of them. If this is done smoothly, it will really baffle the group. Dim the lights, and tell the group that it can only be done on Halloween when the evil spirits are out in force.

### HALLOWEEN I.Q. TEST

If you like taking tests, here's one for Halloween. You could use it in a meeting or at a party, offering a prize (a handful of wet pumpkin seeds?) to whoever gets the most answers correct.

1. Halloween is the eve of
   A. All Hallows
   B. Hallowmas
   C. All Saints Day
   D. All of the above
   E. None of the above

2. The earliest Halloween celebrations were held by
   A. The Druids
   B. The Romans
   C. The Greeks
   D. The French

3. Halloween was held in honor of
   A. Romulus
   B. Som hain, Lord of the Dead
   C. Zeus
   D. Count de Guilloteen

4. What famous historical event occurred on Halloween 1517?

5. The first execution for witchcraft in New England took place in
   A. Connecticut (1650)
   B. Boston (1648)
   C. Salem (1692)
   D. Chicago (1706)

6. An early name for Halloween in North America was
   A. Snap Apple Night
   B. Brotherhood Evening
   C. Hoe Down
   D. Spook and Shake

7. What do you call a hot dog with all the insides taken out?

8. If you lived in a graveyard
   A. How would you open the gate?
   B. What would your disposition be?
   What would you do if:
   C. You got something caught in your throat?
   D. You wanted to put on a play?
   E. You wanted to change some music you wrote?

9. Why is the tombstone way the best way?

Answers:
   1. D
   2. A
   3. B
   4. Martin Luther nailed his 95 theses to the door in Wittenberg, Germany.
   5. B
   6. A
   7. A "hollow-weenie"

8. A: Use a skeleton key
   B: Grave
   C: Start coffiin
   D: Rehearse
   E: Decompose
9. It always sticks up for a man when he's down.

## HALLOWEEN VOLLEYBALL

You can play Halloween volleyball using two types of materials. You could use luminous paint (paint which glows in the dark); paint the ball and the net and play volleyball in the dark. Luminous paint is hard to find, especially in a small city. You could also paint the ball with black light paint and use a black light. A white sheet should be thrown over the net. For best results you will need two black lights, one on each side of the net. Using a beach ball instead of a volleyball will keep the game going more smoothly.

## HALLOWEEN WAX MUSEUM

This is a great idea if you live in a city with a Wax Museum. If you checked with the owner, you could probably talk him into letting your youth group into the Wax Museum after hours. Be sure you have adequate leadership to prevent any possible damage to the Museum. Prior to your visit to the Wax Museum, show the kids one of the many Wax Museum horror films (available from companies like Swank Motion Pictures, 201 S. Jefferson, St. Louis, MO 63122; or Budget Films, 4590 Santa Monica Blvd., Los Angeles, CA 90029), then go to the Museum. You will be surprised how scarry a Wax Museum can be after a film like that.

## HITTIN' THE SACK AT THE HAUNTED SHACK

Chances are there is an old weather-beaten, dilapidated, run-down, "haunted" house or barn somewhere within driving distance of your community. Have an overnight campout inside one of these for a very unusual kind of activity. There should be no electricity, no plumbing (preferably an old outhouse), cobwebs, dirt, and an "atmosphere" suitable for ghost stories and such.

## COFFIN MEASURE

Have one boy volunteer to show the group how to be measured for a coffin. Put a blindfold on him to give him the feeling of being dead. Have the boy lie on a table and begin measuring him. Measure from head to shoulder, from shoulder to hand, from waist to foot. Then lift up his left leg and measure from his leg to hip. Lift his right leg and pour a cup of water down his pant leg.

## CYCLOPS

For this game the group should be divided into teams of three to five and a volunteer should be selected from each group. Give each group a box of materials including tape, newspaper, aluminum foil, cellophane, or other items. On the word "go," the volunteer must be covered completely, except for one eye, by the rest of his/her group (henceforth known as the "pit crew") with the materials. Once the volunteer is completely covered, a referee should check the "cyclops" out, and if no clothing or skin is showing, the cyclops may begin the attack (without interference or assistance from the pit crew). No cyclops may attack without permission from a referee.

The object is to attack, in the form of a "tag," another cyclops who is not yet ready for attack. Once an unprepared cyclops is tagged, he/she is eliminated. The unprepared cyclops may flee the tag, and the pit crew may keep working on him/her while he/she is fleeing. The attacking cyclops may remain in pursuit until a piece of his/her covering falls off and some skin or clothing shows through. If this should occur, the attacker must stop and allow the pit crew to make the necessary repairs. The events should continue until there is only one cyclops left.

## GHOST RACE

This is a wild relay game that can be a lot of fun. Team members are given a sheet with two little eye-holes cut out of it. On a signal, the person must put the sheet over his or her head, get the eye-holes in place (which is not easy when you are in a hurry) and run to a goal and back. The sheet is then passed to the next person who does the same thing. The team that finishes first (all team members completing the task) is the winner. To make the game even more difficult (and rougher), omit the eye-holes in the sheet. Contestants must then run virtually blindfolded back and forth to the goal as teammates yell out directions.

## GHOST WALK

For this spooky game, divide into teams of six to eight people, tied together at the wrist to form a line. Use a long ball of string or yarn to stretch out a course. This is best done in big buildings with many obstacles. Have each team follow their colored yarn wherever it goes without breaking their chain or the yarn. The first team with their yarn completely rolled up and their chain not broken wins. This is especially effective if all lights are off and wandering ghosts are used. You may also want to incorporate spooky music throughout the building.

## GOOBER RELAY

Contestants must line up for this game relay-style. The first person must carry a peanut between their knees to a pumpkin (hollowed out with a hole in the top) and must drop it in. He/she must run back and tag the next team member. They must then run to the pumpkin, take the peanut out and carry it back in the same fashion (between the knees). The next person should repeat the process. First team to finish wins.

## GROTESQUE SCAVENGER HUNT

This crazy scavenger hunt idea can be done at any time during the year, but would probably go over the best during the ghoulish season of Halloween. Like most scavenger hunts, kids are divided into teams and sent out with a list of items to bring back. Here is the list:

1. ¼ cup or more of ketchup
2. 1 raw egg
3. 1 bone (any kind)
4. ¼ cup or more of mustard (or horseradish)
5. ½ cup of leftover vegetables (any kind)
6. ½ cup flour
7. Any portion of jello or pudding
8. Two inches of toothpaste
9. Any portion of leftover meat (any kind)
10. ½ cup of leftover coffee or tea

Each team should be sent out with ten small "zip-lock" plastic sandwich bags that will hold each of the items listed. Each team should also appoint a captain, who must be courageous and daring. The captain can organize the scavenger hunt.

After the teams return with the items on the list, the next stage of the event may begin. The captain should be seated in a chair, in front of a table where there is a bowl. The rest of the team should be about twenty feet away. Each team member must bring one of the bags collected on the scavenger hunt and (one at a time) deposit the contents into the bowl. (The egg must be cracked and the shell thrown away.) After all the contents of all ten bags are in the bowl, the last person must stir the whole mess around ten times, take one big spoonful, and feed it to the team captain. After the captain swallows it, he must stand up and shout, "My compliments to the chef!" The first team to complete this wins.

65

A slightly simpler version of this would be to skip the scavenger hunt and to provide all the ingredients for the teams. That way you would have a little more control over the cleanliness of the food items. Of course if you choose to go with the scavenger hunt, lay down some rules like: only one food item per house may be collected; no item can come from the garbage; and so on.

## HALLOWEEN DINNER

This is a variation of the "Mystery Dinner," in which people order items from a menu without knowing exactly what it is that they are ordering. All the food items as well as the eating utensils have disguised names. A person orders food in three courses, four items per course, from the menu below. A waitress (dressed as a witch) can fill the orders and bring the food to the table. The person must consume each course (all of it) before the next course can be ordered and received. It's a lot of fun and full of surprises. Here's the menu:

"Witches Brew" (Punch)
"Lapover" (napkin)
"Jack's Ripper" (knife)
"Devil's Right Arm" (fork)
"Grave Diggers Delight" (spoon)
"Autumn Nectar" (milk)

"Pig in a Poke" (hot dog)
"Tombstone" (bun)
"Irish Eyes" (fried potatoes)
"Bones" (beans)
"Slimy Shivers" (jello)
"Frosted Pumpkin" (pie)

Some other possible names for items on the menu:

"Goblins Cauldron"
"Haunted Hash"
"Black Cat's Curse"
"Evil Elixer"
"Frankenstein Fu Yung"

"Spider Saute"
"Creepy Crepes"
"Monster Mash"
"Dracula's Dream"
"Frightful Flambe"

### HALLOWEEN HOLIDAY SHOW

As part of a Halloween costume party this year, have a "Holiday Fashion Show." Have certain kids dress up for different holidays of the year. Have somebody in a Lincoln outfit, a workers outfit (for Labor Day), etc. Have a moderator describe each outfit. They should be as humorous as possible. The moderator can also give a little history of the holiday represented. The last one can be Santa Claus, who could have a gift for everyone.

### HALLOWEEN HYSTERIA

Here's a group game or mixer which is great for Halloween. Everyone should be given a sheet with the list below printed on it. They should also get a pencil. On "go," all must try to complete the instructions in any order they wish. When they complete each one, they should have the other person involved initial that particular item. The first to complete the entire list is the winner. To organize the confusion, you might circle a different number (ahead of time) on each sheet. Then announce that the list must be completed in order, beginning with the number that is circled, then back to number 1 after 10.

# HALLOWEEN HYSTERIA

1. Sneak up behind someone, tap their shoulder, and when they turn around, make a face and yell "BOO!" as loud as you can. They initial here _____.

2. Do your best impression of Count Dracula and say to someone: "I want to drink your blood." They initial here _____.

3. Get three people together and SCREAM together for five seconds. One person initials here _____.

4. Find someone with a funny costume and laugh at them for ten seconds while pointing at them. They initial here _____.

5. Go to someone with makeup on and howl like a wolf--three short howls and one long howl. They initial here _____.

6. Find someone who does not have a costume on and say to that person: "Hey, your outfit looks pretty cute!" They initial here _____.

7. Using your own address, tell someone where there is a "haunted house," and show them how to get there by drawing a map on the back of their sheet. They initial here _____.

8. Go to three people and for three long seconds, look like you just saw a ghost and then shout, "I did, I did, I did!" The third person initials here _____.

9. Walk around the room for one minute acting like you are the Great Pumpkin, telling everybody you walk by how much you weigh. Get the last person you tell to initial here _____.

10. Run around and around someone yelling "trick or treat," not letting that person do anything until they give you something (anything). They initial here _____.

## MONSTER MAD LIB

Here's a "Mad Lib" that would be great for your next Halloween party. It's simply a story with key words left out. Assign each of the following directions to individuals in the group and have each one put down the appropriate answer. Each answer is numbered to correspond to its appropriate place in the story. Read the story aloud with the answers offered by the individuals.

1. A number *44*
2. A local high school *central*
3. An adjective *active*
4. A verb *jumped*
5. A person in the group *Shane*
6. A means of transportation *car*
7. A girl in the group *Tara*
8. A room *kitch*
9. A verb *flew*
10. An adjective *big*
11. An adjective *awful*
12. A verb *growth*
13. A noun *book*
14. A toy *slinky*
15. A greeting *hello*
16. An exclamation *hey!*
17. A part of the body *toe*
18. A place or location *gas station*
19. An adjective *ugly*
20. An adjective *blackened*
21. A boy in the group *Derek*
22. A noun *paper*
23. A place *Rolla*
24. A mushy line *I love you, girl!*
25. A part of the body *hand*
26. Your church *Fcco*

*3 goobers*

Once upon a time, ___1___ years ago, in that fiendish place Transylvania (which is now known as _____2_____ ), the ___3___ Count Dracula ___4___-ed. Our story finds him just after he has finished his dinner, which tonight included _____5_____ . Since he was still a little hungry and a full moon was out, he decided to catch the next _____6_____ to ___7___'s house and to peek into her ___8___ to see if she was ___9___-ing. By chance she was, which brought a ___10___ smile to his ___11___ face. Without wasting a second, he ___12___-ed into her ___13___, startling her so much that she broke her ___14___ . "___15___," spake Count Dracula. "I have come to drink your blood!" "___16___ !" she replied, whereupon she kicked Dracula in the _____17_____ and fled. Not to be deterred, Dracula chased her as far as _____18_____ where he finally tackled her. It looked like the end for ___(same girl)___, but just before Dracula could sink his ___19___ fangs into her ___20___ neck, ___21___ arrived on the scene. Quickly sizing up the situation, he grabbed the nearest ___22___ and smote Dracula so hard it was heard in ___23___ . "___24___," sighed ___(same girl)___ . "Aw, it was nothing," replied ___(same boy)___ as he flexed his ___25___ for her. "By the way," he asked. "What's a nice girl like you doing in the _____26_____ high school group?"

## MONSTER MAKE-UP

Select three couples for this event. The boys must sit in chairs facing the audience and the girls must "make-up" the guys with "cosmetics" such as peanut butter, mud, toothpaste, and other messy items. The audience should judge to determine the ugliest.

## MUMMY

Select two or three guys to be "mummified." Each guy should have two girls wrap him up in toilet paper or paper towels from head to toe within a given time limit. The audience should judge to determine the best job.

## THE MURDER OF HERBERT SMEAR

Try this for a shrieking success. Everyone should be seated in a circle with the lights dimmed. A record player on slow speed with a talking or singing record will produce weird sounds. Play such a record, very softly, for a ghostly background effect.

The leader should enter the room draped in a sheet, with a flashlight concealed beneath the sheet in such a way as to throw a light upon his face. Then he should read the following poem, using an ominous voice, pausing at specific times while his assistants pass the articles mentioned.

### THE MURDER OF HERBERT SMEAR

*Listen, my children, and you shall hear*
*About a murder which happened here,*
*Upon a night both dark and drear,*
*To a poor old man called Herbert Smear.*

*I have with me the man's remains.*
*Of them, I pass you now his brains!*
(Pass a moist sponge or a thin plastic bag of cold macaroni)

*His eyes were blue, his skin was fair;*
*And soft and silky was his hair.*
(Pass pieces of fur, corn silk, or a wig)

*An old man, he could barely hear.*
*Caress poor Herbert's deaf old ear*
(Pass dried peaches or apricots)

*As the murderer struck the blow unheard,*
*This windpipe forced out Smear's last word!*
(Pass lengths of uncut, cold, boiled macaroni)

*The ghastly grin of death did wreath*
*This set of gleaming, pearly teeth.*
(Pass kernels of dried corn)

*Slowly, Smear's poor corpse grew cold.*
*I give you now his hand to hold.*
(Pass rubber glove stuffed with cold, wet sand)

*If only Smear had been more wise*
*His head might still contain these eyes.*
(Pass peeled grapes)

*Although they're dry and brittle now,*
*Smear's backbone once made courtly bows.*
(Pass empty spools strung together with string)

*This sound should melt a heart of stone*
*The mournful rattle of Smear's old bones!*
(Chains rattle)

## NEWSPAPER COSTUMES

For this contest you should divide the group up so that there are three people in a group. Each group should be given twelve pieces of newspaper and eight straight pins. The contest is to see which group can make the most original costume, neatness of course counting. It's good to see how much creativity people have. Have a judge choose the winning group.

## PASS THE BONE

Get an old dog bone, tie a string to it, and play the game that requires team members to run the bone through their clothing so that the whole team is hooked together by the string. The bone should be passed up the sleeve, down through the shirt, through a pant leg, and out to the next person, pulling the string along as you go. The first team to be tied together that way wins. The idea of passing a bone through their clothes gives most kids the creeps.

## PING PONG PUMPKIN

For this game, all you need are some Ping Pong balls and a few pumpkins of various sizes. Hollow the pumpkins out, with a hole in the top, and assign a point value to each. Smaller pumpkins should be worth more, bigger pumpkins should be worth less. The idea is to bounce Ping Pong balls into the pumpkins from a distance of about ten feet away. The bigger pumpkins are easier to hit, hence the scoring. Cut the point value of each pumpkin out of the side of the pumpkin. If you play the game at night, darken the room and light the insides of the pumpkins with flashlights.

## PUMPKIN CAROLS

This Halloween, go "Pumpkin Caroling" to peoples' houses, like you would normally do at Christmas. Print up songsheets on orange paper with the following "carols":

*GREAT PUMPKIN IS COMIN' TO TOWN*
Oh, you better not shriek, you better not groan,
You better not howl, you better not moan.
Great Pumpkin is comin' to town!

He's going to find out from folks that he meets
Who deserves tricks and who deserves treats.
Great Pumpkin is comin' to town!

He'll search in every pumpkin patch,
Haunted houses far and near,
To see if you've been spreading gloom
Or bringing lots of cheer.

So, you better not shriek, you better not groan,
You better not howl, you better not moan.
Great Pumpkin is comin' to town!

*THE TWELVE DAYS OF HALLOWEEN*

On the twelfth day of Halloween
My true love gave to me
Twelve bats a-flying,
Eleven masks a-leering,
Ten ghouls a-grooming,
Nine ghosts a-booing,
Eight monsters shrieking,
Seven pumpkins glowing,
Six goblins bobbling,
Five scary spooks,
Four skeletons,
Three black cats,
Two trick-or-treaters,
And an owl in a dead fir tree.

*I HEARD THE BELLS ON HALLOWEEN*

I heard the bells on Halloween
Their old, familiar carols scream.
And wild and sweet the words repeat
The pumpkin season's here again.

Then pealed the bells more loud and strong,
Great Pumpkin comes before too long.
The good will get, the bad will fret.
The pumpkin season's here again.

71

*PUMPKIN WONDERLAND*

Screech owls hoot, are you list-nin?
'Neath the moon, all is glist-nin'—
A real scary sight, we're happy tonight,
Waitin' in a pumpkin wonderland.

In the patch we're waitin' for Great Pumpkin,
We've been waiting for this night all year.
For we've tried to be nice to everybody
And to grow a pumpkin patch that is sincere!

Later on, while we're eating
What we got trick-or-treating,
We'll share all our sacks of Halloween snacks,
Waiting in a pumpkin wonderland.

*I'M DREAMING OF THE GREAT PUMPKIN*

I'm dreaming of the Great Pumpkin
Just like I do this time each year.
When he brings nice toys to good girls and boys
Who wait for him to appear.

I'm dreaming of the Great Pumpkin
With every pumpkin card I write.
May your jack-o-lanterns burn bright
When the Great Pumpkin visits you tonight.

*PUMPKIN BELLS*

Dashing through the streets
In our costumes bright and gay.
To each house we go
Laughing all the way.
Halloween is here,
Making spirits bright,
What fun it is to trick-or-treat
And sing pumpkin carols tonight!

Oh . . . pumpkin bells, pumpkin bells,
Ringing loud and clear.
Oh what fun Great Pumpkin brings
When Halloween is here!

## PUMPKIN CARVING

Give each team a whole pumpkin and a couple of knives. On a signal, each team should try to come up with the most creative pumpkin they can. Awards can be given for best job, most humorous, ugliest, scariest, and so on. Big pumpkins work best.

One thing that is fun to do with this is to have each team select a "team captain." Then the judges decide which pumpkin is the worst. The team captain responsible for that pumpkin will get all of the insides of the pumpkins (seeds, etc.) dumped on his or her head.

## PUMPKIN PARTNERS

Here's a good way to get kids into teams. From cardboard cut out some pumpkin-shaped puzzles like the diagram below. There should be as many pumpkins as there are going to be teams. Each puzzle should be different, so that when the puzzle pieces are randomly distributed, the kids must find others who have parts of the same pumpkin. The first team to get a completed pumpkin put together is the winner.

## PUMPKIN PIE PARTY

Instead of a scavenger hunt, go on a pumpkin pie–making mission. Divide into groups of four or five. Give each group a pie plate, a recipe for making a pumpkin pie, and a few empty cans and bags to hold the collected ingredients. Have them go around from door to door asking for one of the ingredients listed. (If the recipe requires three eggs, they should go to three houses) You can decide whether to make and bake the pies when you return.

## PUMPKIN PUSH

Here's a good game for your next Halloween Party. Divide the group into several teams. Give each team a pumpkin of the same approximate size. Place a chair (one for each team) about twenty feet away from the team. If you have four teams, use four chairs. The object is for each person on the team to push the pumpkin around his team's chair and back to the next player. The first team to have all of its players finish is the winner. The catch is this: the players may only use their pelvises to push the pumpkins while doing a "crab walk" sideways. Or you may have them push the pumpkins with their heads. For added excitement and chaos, have two or three teams going around the same chair.

## SCARECROW STUFF

This game works great for a Halloween party or a hayride where plenty of hay or straw is available. Divide the kids into two teams or more, depending on the size of the group. Each team should have an equal size pile of hay before them. Each team should choose a person to serve as the team's "scarecrow." The "scarecrows" must stand the same distance away wearing oversized overalls. The object will be to see which team can use up all the hay in stuffing their scarecrow. For added laughs have the scarecrows finish the race by running to a certain finish line.

## SCARY SCAVENGER HUNT

Here's a scavenger hunt that could be done on Halloween. Some of the items below are somewhat vague, making it necessary for the kids to be creative in order to bring back something that might fit the description. You can add more to this list.

A witch's eye (this could be a marble, etc.)
A popcorn ball
A bat's wing (this could be a chicken wing, etc.)
A voodoo doll (complete with pins)
Two feet of black streamers
A popped orange balloon
Any mask (the scariest wins)
Four pieces of "chicken corn" candy
A dozen pumpkin seeds
Black cat fur
A bar of soap for someone's window
A signature from someone (not in your group) who believes in ghosts.

## SCREAM IN THE DARK

Have a screaming contest. Judge to see who can scream the loudest, longest, highest, most blood-curdling, etc. For effect, do it with the lights out. For a prize or an award furnish ice cream. (Baskin-Robbins usually has a black and orange variety around Halloween.)

## SPOOK'S SPREE

This is an old-fashioned "Halloween Carnival" that features a variety of booths set up around the room (or outdoors) with a different game in each and the opportunity for people to try and win prizes, etc. You can charge a certain amount per game, or you could give kids a ticket book with each ticket good for one try at a game. Some sample games:

1. *The Cat's Meow:* Roll a ping pong ball through an open cylinder (paper towel tube) and try to make it land in a flat pie tin.

2. *Apple Fish:* Tie a string with a weight onto a fishing pole and have the kids cast it through holes in the back of the booth. Apples should be tied on and the string pulled back out.

3. *Ring Toss:* Chairs turned upside down provide four poles. Toss clothes hangers over them.

4. *Bean Bag:* Paint figures on the back of a booth with holes in the figures. Bean bags should be thrown through the holes.

5. *Plate Sailing:* Use four rinsed-out ice cream containers (large, can type) and have kids toss paper plates into them frisbee-style.

6. *Down the Hatch:* Drop clothespins into small containers or bottles.

7. *Pumpkin Bowling:* Set up plastic containers and roll a small or medium sized ball at them.

8. *Owling Inn:* Use small metal wastebaskets tilted against the wall at a 45-degree angle. Players get ten Ping Pong balls and should try to bounce them in.

9. *Shot in the Dark:* Allow three squirts of a water pistol at a row of lighted candles. Only one candle needs to be extinguished.

10. *Ghost Hunt:* Hang white dishcloths on a corkboard surface and pin balloons on the dishcloths (in the center). Use a black light and the balloons will show up as dark spots on the white surface. Throw darts at the balloons.

11. *Ping Pong Pumpkin:* Have kids toss Ping Pong balls into pumpkins lighted by flashlights inside.

12. *Jack O'Luck:* Make a jack o'lantern face cutout of a cardboard box and toss rubber balls in through the holes. Light the inside of the box with flashlights.

13. *Peanut Pitch:* Throw peanuts onto a large outline of a peanut drawn on the floor. Peanuts which fall within the outline win.

14. *Tic Tac Throw:* Throw bean bags onto a table which has a large tic-tac-toe diagram on it. Three in a row wins.

15. *Pumpkin Looping:* Use coat hangers made into a circle or plastic hoops to toss around pumpkins.

16. *Squirt Box:* Kids are given squirt guns (or pies, etc.) and get a chance to let their favorite youth sponsor or parent have it.

Make up some games of your own or use some of the many games used at commercial carnivals (tossing pennies onto plates, knocking over stuffed animals with baseballs, etc.).

## TRICK OR TREAT RELAY

Divide into teams and have them line up single file. Some distance away from the front of each team should be a "trick or treat" sack (paper bag) full of "goodies." Each team member must run to the bag, yell out "Trick or Treat," reach into the bag (without looking), and eat whatever she pulls out. After eating the item, she may then run back to the team and tag the next player, who must do the same thing. Use your own creativity when it comes to selecting items for the bag. Some suggestions:

A green onion
A walnut (without a nut cracker)
A jar of baby food and spoon attached
Prunes
A lemon
A warm can of pop

Cream cheese (wrapped in waxed paper)
A peanut butter sandwich
A sardine

## SPOOK INSURANCE

Sell "insurance policies" at Halloween to families in the church to protect them from having to clean up after the usual pranks that go along with the ghoulish holiday. Triple the price for businesses. Since most home owners never need cleanup services, it is clear profit and a good fund raiser. (Make sure you have some kids to do the work in case it is needed, however.)

---

### SPOOK INSURANCE

Policy 1: Grass Plat—This policy protects your lawn against such disasters as being strewn with candy wrappers, rocks, rotten eggs, water balloon particles, T.P. (toiler paper), etc.

Policy 2: Diaphanous—This policy will protect your windows against usery—i.e. graffiti, wax, soap, eggs, and other foreign materials. (Does not cover breakage!)

---

Please fill out the following information.

Name _____ Phone _____

Address _____

Policy 1: GRASS PLAT (Lawn mess)          Price: $ .75 _____

Policy 2: DIAPHANOUS (Window mess)        Price: $ .75 _____
Policy 3: COMBINATION OF 1 and 2          Price: $1.50 _____

Please report claims to the church before 9:00 p.m. on Wednesday, November 3.

---

## THREE TERRIBLE FATES

This is a good game for small groups in a casual setting. The group should sit in a circle. To begin, each person should think of something really terrible that might happen to someone, like "You'll be bitten by a black widow spider and die." They then must tell the person on their right what their terrible fate is. Next, they must think of where this terrible fate might happen, like "In an outhouse." They should tell the person on their left this information. The group then exchanges seats (mixes up). After this each person thinks of who might be with them when this terrible fate occurs, like "The entire starting backfield of the Green Bay Packers." Each person must tell this information to the person on his right. Lastly, each person should think of when this terrible fate might happen, like ''During the Sunday morning sermon.'' This should be told to the person on the left. Now everyone has been told *what* their fate is, *where* it will happen, *who* they will be with, and *when* it will occur. Go around the circle and have everyone tell all about their terrible fate. It's a lot of fun. If the above is too scary for your group, change it to something like who, where, when, etc., you will meet your sweetheart.

## THE UGLIEST MONSTER IN THE WORLD

Bring in a guy with a blanket over his head who will be the ''monster.'' Tell everybody that this monster is so ugly that anyone who looks at him falls over dead. Three guys in the audience (clued-in) should come up to try. They will look under the blanket and sure enough, they will fall over dead. Now choose a girl (unsuspecting) to come up and look under the blanket, just to prove that girls are the stronger sex. She will come up, look under the blanket, and when she does . . . the monster will fall dead.

## THE UNKNOWN SPOOK

This game is good when you have a group that doesn't know each other well. Give everyone a paper sack that will fit over their heads properly. There should also be enough drawing tools (pens, crayons, etc.) on hand for everyone. Have everyone go somewhere in the room and punch out eye holes, mouth holes, etc. Then they should draw a face on the sack. This can be just a simple drawing, nothing fancy. The lights should be turned off, and everyone must put on their masks. When the lights are turned back on, the crowd should begin milling around. Each person must approach another and challenge that person to guess her identity. If she is wrong, that person (who guessed wrong) must autograph the other's sack while it is still on her head. If she is correct, then she must put an ''X'' on the sack. When a person gets five (or any number you choose) ''X's'' on her sack, she is out of the game. Whoever gets the most autographs wins. That person should be introduced to the group.

## WHERE TO GET HORROR MOVIES

Halloween is a great time to show horror or monster movies. Usually you will need to reserve them well in advance if you intend to show one at your Halloween event. Be sure and check with your public library, as they will often have some of the classic Frankenstein, Dracula, Wolfman, etc. films. Other good film sources include:

Budget Films
4590 Santa Monica Blvd.
Los Angeles, CA 90029

Swank Films
6767 Forest Lawn Dr.
Hollywood, CA 90068

Films, Inc.
5625 Hollywood Blvd.
Hollywood, CA 90028

Audio Brandon Films
1619 N. Cherokee
Los Angeles, CA 90028

## WITCH HUNT (or GREAT PUMPKIN HUNT)

This is a variation of the old "Treasure Hunt," in which people follow "clues" to reach a treasure. The difference here is the object of the hunt, namely a witch. The witch should be a dummy dressed up like a witch, hidden somewhere in town. Kids should be divided into teams, each team traveling together, either in a car or a bus. Each team must start out with the same clue, and the clues will lead the team to further clues and then finally to the witch. All the clues should be written to give a "witchy" feeling; such as, "With this clue, you'll get your start. Look for a 'stake' to drive through her heart." This clue might send the kids to a local steak house, etc., depending on how you set it up. Don't make the clues too easy. After a team finds the witch, they must bring it back to the meeting place to win, so put the witch where it's hard to get. Up in a tree, under a house, in the middle of a shopping center are all good locations. When the witch is brought in, burn it at the stake, show some horror movies, or have a Halloween Party.

Another variation of this would be to have a "Great Pumpkin Hunt." Have the group build a giant pumpkin out of paper mache, or purchase a large pumpkin that can be hidden somewhere in the area. Kids can then follow clues in the same manner as described above. The team that gets to the Great Pumpkin first and brings it back will be the winner.

## WITCH SKIT

This skit requires two people. One is dressed up like a "witch," with the usual witch-looking apparel: a black hat and dress, long crooked nose, scraggly wig (an old mop will do), and a broom. The other is an average but good-looking young man who is extremely depressed and is about to commit suicide. As the skit begins, we find him ready to "end it all."

| Man: | I can't take it any longer! I've lost my family, my job, my friends, and my house burned down. Life is not worth living! I'm going to end it all right now . . . (etc.) |
|---|---|
| Witch: | (Enters, speaks in a squeaky voice.) What are you doing, young man? Ha-ha-ha-hee-hee-hee (And other witch-like sounds.) |
| Man: | Life just isn't worth living. I've lost all my friends, family, job, and all my possessions, and now I'm going to jump off this cliff and end it all. |
| Witch: | Oh no, don't do that. |
| Man: | Why shouldn't I? |
| Witch: | Because, tee-hee, I'm a witch with magic powers and I can give you back everything you lost and more! I'll grant you three wishes! Tee-hee-hee! Three wishes!!! |
| Man: | You mean that you can give me three wishes? Wow, that would be tremendous! I wouldn't have to end it all! . . . Wait a minute. How do I know that you are telling me the truth? How do I know that you are really a witch? |
| Witch: | Of course, I'm a witch. Don't I *look* like a witch? Ha-ha-ha-hee-hee-hee. I'll give you your three wishes in exchange for one small favor. |
| Man: | One favor? (Skeptical) I knew there must be a catch. What do you want from me? |
| Witch: | Three kisses. It's a fair exchange. Three wishes for three kisses! |
| Man: | I think I'll just jump anyway. |
| Witch: | Think of all you'll be able to wish for in three wishes! |
| Man: | (He finally decides to go ahead with it, so he takes the witch in his arms and begins to kiss her. After each kiss, the young man makes repulsive gestures, spitting each time. Extreme distaste is shown after the last kiss, and with it a great sigh of relief. The witch, on the other hand, shows extreme enjoyment with each kiss, smiling and making little squeals of pleasure each time she is kissed.) Okay, now that that is over, I want my three wishes. |
| Witch: | First of all, tell me how old you are, sonny. |
| Man: | (He tells her his age.) |
| Witch: | And you still believe in witches at that age??? Ha-ha-ha-hee-hee-hee . . . (She exits, cackling to herself.) |

# Creative Communication

### THE GOSPEL PUMPKIN

For a more "positive" approach to Halloween, have your youth group carve messages in jack-o-lanterns, rather than the traditional pumpkin face. A few suggestions: "Peace," "Love," "God is Love," "Smile," etc.

### HALLOWEEN GIVE-AWAY

This idea not only benefits the community and the church, but will really leave an impression on your young people.

This Halloween have each young person bring a costume and a pound of Halloween candy. Have a number of empty paper bags prepared. After the kids arrive in costume, instruct them to open their candy and divide it equally among the empty bags. Then add to the bags several good pieces of literature which could include things like an introductory brochure about the church, a letter from the youth (see example), and a modern translation New Testament.

HAPPY HALLOWEEN!

The 'scary-looking' bunch that just rang your doorbell, shouting 'trick-or-treat' are members of the local _____ church's youth group.

We wanted to take this rather unique opportunity to celebrate Halloween with your family in ways other than soaping your windows, TPing your trees, or asking you for candy. We wanted to be able to share with you this Halloween.

So we put together these little 'goodie bags.' Candy for the children, and some interesting little booklets for everyone. It is our hope that this little 'goodie bag' will be enjoyed by everyone in your family.

We hope that as you eat the candy, you will take time to look through some of the booklets. They contain some 'good things,' too.

Have a happy Halloween. We have enjoyed this opportunity to talk with you and want you to know that our church is especially interested in your family. If you don't already attend a church regularly, we would love to have you attend our services. If there is ever any way we can be of assistance to you and your loved ones, please feel free to call us.

God bless you all!

We would suggest that you might find it effective if you not only let the kids know what you were planning but encouraged them to give their own money to buy the candy and the books. It would probably mean more to them.

## I FEAR MOST

Here's a good discussion starter that works well around Halloween. Divide into small groups and discuss the following questions:

1. What was the most frightening experience you've ever had?
2. What were you afraid of most when you were younger?
3. What are you afraid of most now?
4. Is fear good or bad?
5. Rate these fears in order of intensity for you. In other words, put the one you fear most at the top, and the one you fear least at the bottom.
   a. fear of heights
   b. fear of the future
   c. fear of failing
   d. fear of what the crowd thinks of me
   e. fear of God
   f. fear of death
   g. fear of the dark
   h. fear of _____

Following the last question, have kids share the results of question #5 with each other (optional) and tell why they listed them as they did. You can follow this up with a study of fear from Scripture and other guidelines on how to overcome fear through faith in Christ. Have the kids learn 2 Timothy 1:7, which reads, "For God did not give us a spirit of fear, but a spirit of power and love and self-control."

## SIN BURIAL

This exercise would be good for a serious conclusion to a Halloween Party. Have the kids write down a sin, a problem, or something preventing them from being close to God. Have a "funeral procession" to a prearranged site, dig a grave (complete with a marker), and have the kids toss their "sins" into the grave with a prayer of commitment. Cover the grave and the marker can remain as a permanent reminder of this commitment.

## TOMBSTONE TREASURE HUNT

A lot of kids are sheltered from the reality of death. Many have never been faced with death in the family, and some have never even attended a funeral. The purpose of this idea is not to scare young people but to help them realize that death is real, and that all of us who are born will someday die. Here is an unusual but effective way to get kids thinking about death for a serious discussion.

The leader should go to a cemetery in advance and make out fifteen to twenty questions that can be answered by looking at the gravestones. For example:

1. What state is William R. Baline, PFC, 66 Quartermaster Co. from?
2. Who was "Lost to memory! Lost to love! Who has gone to our Father's house above"?
3. How old was Diane M. Ferrell?
4. What Scripture reference is on Richard Keith's stone?

Make enough copies of the questions for everyone in your group. Take the kids to the cemetery and have them look at the stones to find the answers. (Get permission from the cemetery before doing this.) They may want to go in small groups. Some may be scared by the idea and just want to stay by the car. Tell them to remember where they are and to stay away from any mourners. Encourage them to do the activity but don't push them if they are really frightened. When the kids are finished or the time is up, gather them in a clear spot in or near the cemetery for a discussion. (Cemeteries are nice quiet places for discussions.) Go over the answers to the questions just for fun, then begin a discussion about their feelings. Some starter questions are:

1. How did the game make you feel?
2. What did you think about the people whose stones you were reading?
3. What would you want written on your own tombstone?
4. What bothers you the most about death?
5. Have you ever thought about your own death?

Conclude with some remarks about death being the natural end to life here on earth, something that happens to everyone. We don't have to be afraid of death. John 6:47

is a good Scripture to use in building some thoughts about the Christian's triumph over death. Remind them that God loves them, and that He is preparing a place for His children. Also remind them what is promised to sinners but resist the temptation to sell fire insurance at this point. This activity and discussion will get kids thinking not only about death, but about how to make their lives count.

## TRICK OR TREATING FOR OTHERS

As a service project, have your youth group canvas the neighborhood in costumes and with paper bags, asking people to donate food items for needy families. It's a nice change of pace for most people who are already expecting people at their door anyway. A variation of this would be to go ahead and collect "treats," just like everyone else, but to inform people at each house that these treats are being collected to give to children who are unable to go trick or treating themselves, like those in hospitals, etc. Of course, you should know ahead of time who you are collecting the food for, and how it is going to be distributed. It might be fun to visit the hospital, etc., while in costume to distribute the candy or food.

## TREATS MAKING PARTY

Have your youth group spend an evening making popcorn balls, fudge, cookies, and other treats. Then on Halloween have them deliver the treats to an orphanage, hospital, or home.

# The Spook House

This section contains some great ideas and special effects for a "Spook House" that can be used at Halloween. Some of them are easy to do; others are a bit more complex. But they are all guaranteed to be fun and really scary, without being gory or bordering on the occult. If you do go to all the trouble and/or expense to put together a good spook house, keep it open for several nights and promote it well. A small admission charge will help cover your costs and perhaps raise some additional money for your group or for other worthwhile needs.

## RAIN EFFECT

*Materials:* Large Styrofoam ball or wig head, glue, small mirror pieces (or pieces from broken mirror), ten-to-twenty-RPM motor, light.

Glue the mirror pieces all over the styrofoam. Mount the ball onto the motor so that it will rotate vertically. Aim a tiny spot of light onto the rotating ball in a dark room, and the projected spots of light will look like rain. The best way to get the right light is to use a slide projector with the bulb dimmed down. Poke pinholes into a 2" x 2" cardboard piece and project the cardboard onto the ball like a slide. Focus so that the points of light emanating from the device are in focus on the wall of the room.

## FIREFLIES

*Materials:* Very tiny bulbs that run on batteries (check Radio Shack or an electronics store), very thin bell wire, flashlight batteries or a lantern battery, black posterboard, box fan.

It's easy to make the electronic blinking fireflies that Disneyland uses in "Pirates of the Caribbean." Attach the bulb to some eight-foot strands of bell wire and connect them to the battery. A six-volt battery may be too bright; you can tape two "D" size flashlight batteries together (for 3 volts) and attach one wire to each end. Make a small cone-shaped cover for the bulb with black posterboard (see diagram). Hang the bulb from the ceiling so that the bulb is about four feet from the floor. Place the box fan underneath the bulb so that it blows upward. The paper cover over the bulb will catch the fan's breeze and make the bulb dance around from the thin springy wire. It will also make the bulb appear to blink on and off as it momentarily shields the light from view.

The effect in a darkened room is that of a firefly darting about with its tiny light blinking on and off at random. The wires are so thin they are invisible in a darkened room. Mount the firefly behind a window or in a suitable spot where no one can get close enough to figure out how it's done.

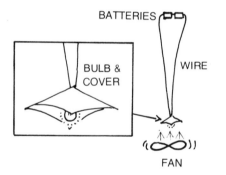

## ROLLING TUNNEL

Find four old doors the same width, and nail them together along their edges to form a tunnel. Screw or bolt four wheels on the bottom side. When a victim crawls into the tunnel, some assistants can begin spinning it around.

## GHOST EFFECT

This has to be the ultimate in baffling optical effects. It's a very simple principle, inexpensive and easy to make, yet very few people can figure it out. Disneyland uses the effect a great deal in the "Haunted Mansion" with their three-dimensional, see-through ghosts that can vanish at will. The applications are limitless and unreal.

You can make talking statues, ghosts rising out of solid coffins, floating hands, small displays, or life-size ghosts. *Keep the technique top secret from your teens.*

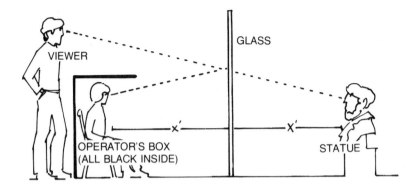

The principle is that of virtual images, and the main ingredient is a sheet of glass. The size of the glass depends on how big your display will be. If you have access to a large window pane or store-front glass, you're in business.

Let's say you want to create a "Talking Statue." Pick out a life-size plaster bust at a statuary store (or you can use a styrofoam wig head). Mount the statue right where you want it. Make a peep hole for the viewer at least six feet from the statue. Mount your glass (a 3' x 4' pane or larger would be good) about half-way between the viewer and the statue but a little closer to the statue. Build a compartment for the operator right underneath the viewer, and paint the inside flat black. *Important:* everything on the viewer's side of the glass must be black except what you want to show up as a ghost effect. Mount a spotlight so that it will shine directly onto the operator's face only. It's best to connect the light to a dimmer switch, so it can be brought up gradually.

The glass now acts partly as a mirror. Have the operator sit (hidden, of course, from the viewer's sight) so that when the light is on his face, the reflection of his face lines up exactly with the statue's face. He must be exactly the same distance on his side of the glass as the statue is on the other side. When he is in just the right position, the effect is foolproof—no matter where the viewer moves his head to get a better look, he will still see a living face on a stone statue. Practice dimming and brightening the light so that the effect is just right. The operator can yawn as he fades the light up and appear to be "waking up." The operator can even talk to the viewer, calling him by name, and the sound will seem to come from the statue because it, too, will bounce off the glass. Use an operator whose face and voice the people do not recognize. (You could also use a recorded voice and have the operator mouth the words.) To keep the operator's face in just the right position, cut an oval in a piece of plywood, paint the plywood black, and mount it in just the right place. When the operator puts his face in the oval, it will be in just the right position.

Keep the glass crystal clean and do all you can to conceal its edges. The viewer should have no idea any glass is there. Control where the viewer can go so that he cannot come around the side and see how it's done. The novelty of this effect is spoiled if the secret gets out. The possibilities of this technique are limited only by your imaginations; following are some sample applications.

1. *Ghosts:* Make a large-size black compartment for your operators. (You will need a large sheet of glass.) Decorate a living room scene. Create some ghosts dressed in white and have their faces and hands painted black. When the lights come on the ghost operators, they can appear and disappear in your living room set. A "real" person in the living room set can have a ghost sneak up behind her, and she can turn around, scream, and faint. Think up a skit to go with the effect. The viewers need to be above and behind the black box where the ghosts are, looking over the box, through the glass, and into the living room set. They will be amazed at seeing your ghosts walk through solid objects.

2. *Floating hands:* Dress two operators all in black, with white gloves on. Use a black light in the black box to illuminate the gloves. Set a trunk with the lid open out behind the glass on your "stage." The hands can appear to rise right out of the trunk and float around the room, doing strange things. It adds to the effect when you can make the viewer really think and believe that the hands are out there. For instance, put a lamp on your stage and give a remote switch to the operator. The hand can float over to the lamp and appear to turn on the lamp. Another idea: set a small candle (the kind in a glass jar) inside the operator's compartment in just the right position so that its reflection off the glass makes it appear to be sitting on a table in the set. Then the floating hands can pick up the candle, carry it around, and appear to place it back on the table. Your floating hands can juggle, do magic tricks, and really baffle the viewers.

3. *Coffin Trick:* Place a wooden coffin in a mortuary setting. Two ladies should come into the mortuary, look into the coffin, and see a body (a stuffed dummy). They should scream, close the lid, and latch it tight. Then the viewer can watch in surprise as the body rises right through the lid and chases them away. Your operator must be lined up in his black compartment at the same distance from the glass as the coffin on the far side. He should lie down behind a black barrier equal to the side of the coffin. When he sits up, he will appear to sit up right through the lid of the coffin.

4. *Miniature Display:* With smaller glass, you can make a motorized ghost display. Build a box with a peephole and create your scene the same way, with the real ghosts hidden from view and their reflections creating virtual images in the scene. You can use dolls dressed up as ghosts, mounted on small record turntables or with other motors.

5. *Ugly Face in the Mirror:* A girl in your set can be sitting at a mirror combing her hair. Suddenly an ugly face will appear as her reflection and she should scream. Your ghost operator can sit in the black box so that his head appears to be in the mirror. He should wear an ugly mask and turn the light on his face at a certain time. Have the mirror in the set at such an angle that the viewer cannot see a reflection into your secret black compartment.

*Note:* Your virtual-image glass does not have to be perpendicular to the viewer if space is limited. You can stand it up at an angle and have the operator off to one side.

## DR. JEKYLL AND MR. HYDE

This effect is similar to the ghost effect but allows you to merge one scene into another. Build an L-shaped compartment as in the diagram, with the glass at a 45-degree angle to the viewer. Make the two compartments as identical as possible. Connect dimmer switches to the lights in both compartments. (Note: The light in Mr. Hyde's compartment will have to be a higher wattage. Use dim lighting and colored bulbs.) Put an actor dressed up as a mad scientist in Jekyll's compartment with an assortment of test tubes, flasks with colored water and dry ice, books, etc. Put an actor dressed up as ghoulish Mr. Hyde in the other compartment and have the two sitting in *identical positions* and *distances* from the glass. A third person out of view should operate the dimmers.

The effect will be like this: Dr. Jekyll should be sitting in his lab, concocting a bubbling potion. He should drink it, burp, and sit back in his chair with a glazed look. (Operator will begin to fade him out and Mr. Hyde in.) Gradually, right before the viewer's eyes, he will turn into a horrible monster. Mr. Hyde will wake up, feel his head, look in a mirror, groan, and the lights will go out.

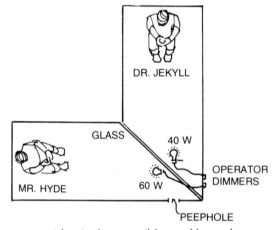

Make the two compartments as identical as possible, and have the actors practice so that they will be in just the right positions when the change occurs. An appropriate musical background on tape can help the actors cue their actions to each other. Of course, this same technique can be used for many other skits.

## SOUND EFFECTS

Borrow cassette players from your young people in advance. Record sound effects from records onto cassettes. Disney's "Chilling, Thrilling Sounds of the Haunted House" has some good sounds—thunder and rain, screams and groans, creaks, etc. To avoid the problem of having to turn cassettes over, buy some TDK Endless Cassettes, which form a continuous loop and repeat over and over. They may be available at a well-stocked electronics store, or the store manager can order them. They come in half-minute, one-, two-, three-, six-, or twenty-minute lengths.

## MAGIC MIRROR

Decorate a wall with a large oval mirror frame and a pane of glass instead of a mirror. Coat the glass with a sheet of aluminized window reflector (available at hardware stores), making the glass into a two-way mirror. Put an operator behind the glass in a darkened compartment, with a dim green bulb in his compartment and a bright light on the viewer's side, connected by dimmer switches.

The viewer will look into the mirror and see only his own reflection when the light is on his side. The operator (dressed in black except for a white face) should dim down the viewer's light and turn up the green light on his face. The viewer then will see the face in the magic mirror talking to him.

Give the mirror operator some good lines to say. He can watch the viewer very well. The light on his own face looks especially gruesome when shining up from beneath. Mount the dimmer switches so that he can operate them easily by hand.

## THUNDER AND LIGHTNING

For a loud, chilling thunder sound, obtain a large piece of sheet metal (about the size of a door). It should be quite flexible. Drill two holes along one long edge and hang it from the ceiling with sturdy wire. When hit in the center with a rubber mallet, it creates an effective thunder sound that rolls for several seconds.

An electronic flash unit for a camera makes an effective lightning flash. To make the victim really get the full effect, use the hot seat.

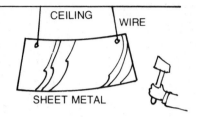

CEILING — WIRE

SHEET METAL

## THE CLAW

Cut out a shape from heavy cardboard like the figure shows. Mount it on the shaft of a one- to four-RPM motor. Place a dim spotlight behind it in such a way that the shape casts a large shadow on a wall. It will look like the shadow of a giant hand coming down.

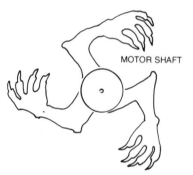

MOTOR SHAFT

If you can't find motors at a large electronics supply, try a barbecue-spit motor or get a catalog from Edmund Scientific Co., 7776 Edscorp Bldg., Barrington, NJ 08007.

## HAUNTED PAINTINGS

Using the principle of parallax, you can create some simple portrait paintings with eyes that stare at you no matter where you stand. They follow you as you walk by. Have an artistic person paint a classic-looking portrait with a stern expression. Cut out the eyes (not the lids, just the part of the eyeball that shows). Paint two pupils of eyes on white poster board the same distance apart as the eyes on the painting.

Mount these pupils about one inch *behind* the painting so that they show through the cut-out holes. When you have it just right, the effect is beautiful.

Lighting is important; mount a separate dim light (a single Christmas tree bulb works well) behind the painting to illuminate the eyes. Aim another bulb with a reflector directly at the front of the painting. Choose wattage and color that will make the best effect.

## AUTOMATIC SWITCHING

There are several ways to have a victim activate a switch that will turn on a light, a siren, an electronic flash, a buzzer, etc. The best is an electronic eye switch sold at Radio Shack for about forty dollars. Cheaper methods will do, however. Most hardware stores with an electrical department sell momentary switches that activate a circuit only when pressed. The trick is to mount the switch so that the victim will step on it and turn on the siren, or whatever you have. One way is to make a short staircase with one collapsing stair that falls about an inch when stepped on and pushes the button. Or else, build a wooden device as shown. The foam rubber springs the top board into position so that the button is only pushed when the board is stepped on.

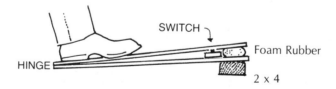

SWITCH

Foam Rubber

HINGE

2 x 4

For an electronic flash, you don't need a button switch; run two wires from the flash tripper (not the AC cord—that should be plugged in separately) to the stepping board. Connect one wire to some aluminum foil stapled to the underside of the top board and the other wire to foil on the bottom board. When stepped on, the two foil pieces will contact and set off the flash. Sirens can be obtained from J. C. Whitney Auto Parts catalog: 1917-19 Archer Ave., P.O. Box 8410, Chicago, IL 60680.

## ACE FROM OUTER SPACE COSTUME

Make a large pillowcase about 2' x 3½' by sewing together three sides of two pieces of sheet that size. Paint a big, ugly face on one side. Your actor should grab his hands above his head, so that when you slip the thing over him, his elbows will be in the top corners. Then get a shirt and stuff the arms with newspaper and pin gloves on for hands. Fasten the collar around his waist, so that his waist appears to be the neck. Fasten a pair of shortened pants around his knees (elasticized pants work well). He will look like a monster with a small body and a huge head.

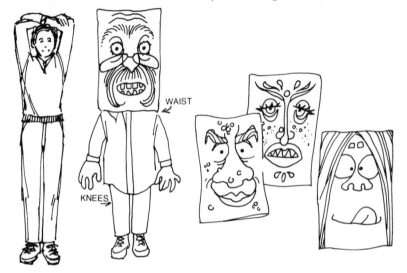

## SPIDER

You can make a spider that automatically drops down in front of a victim. Buy a rubber spider from a toy store and some fish line. Run the fish line from the spider's back up to the ceiling, through an eye screw, and to a door that opens *away* from the spider. When the door is open all the way, the spider should be at the ceiling. When the door closes, the spider will drop down. Get a spring door closer to make the door shut automatically and adjust it so that it closes slowly.

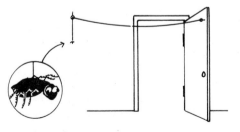

## JACOB'S LADDER SPARK APPARATUS

For your mad-scientist lab, a Jacob's ladder is always impressive. The main ingredient is a heavy-duty ballast that activates large neon signs, if you can find one. Run two wires from the terminals and mount them on a board as shown. Connect the "ground" wire securely to a cold water pipe. *Important:* to prevent shock, keep away from the unit and place it so no one will accidentally get too close. When switched on, sparks begin at the bottom where the two wires are closest together, and travel up the wires one after another. You may need to adjust the wires several times to get them in just the right position where it will work, but be sure it is *OFF* when you touch it. Do not use it for long periods, as it generates ozone. Use a remote switch so you can turn it on from a safe distance.

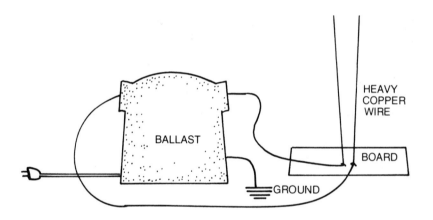

## MOVING DUMMIES

One of the scariest sensations is to walk into a dimly-lit room of a spook house where there are several dummies sitting around on chairs and couches, and you're not sure if they are real people or not. You *know* one of them is going to jump at you, but you can't tell which is for real. The dummies can be made from stuffed clothing pinned together, complete with gloves, shoes, etc. Use wig heads and masks. Have one or two real people dressed similarly. For animation, connect fishline to the hand of a dummy, run it up to the ceiling, through an eye screw, across the ceiling to another eye screw, and down to the real person. Tie the line to a stick so that with a flick of the wrist, the operator can pull on the line and make the dummy's arm raise up. When the victim is looking at the dummy that just moved, the real person can jump up from behind and growl. Fishlines running through eye screws or pulleys can activate many inanimate objects in a fun house. Another example: mount a gorilla mask and a glove on the inside of a door so that it looks like he is peeking out a doorway. When you pull on the line connected to the door, the gorilla will appear to be coming out into the room.

## THE ESCAPED GORILLA

In your fun house, place a guy in a gorilla costume behind a doorway, with large wood dowels in the doorway like prison bars. The victim will feel he is safe, because the gorilla will be behind bars. But then have the gorilla push out the bars and come after him. It's even better if the victim is locked in a room with no way out.

The same idea works with a madman behind bars. After the victim passes by, the madman will quietly slip out of his cell, come up from behind, and put his hand on the victim's shoulder.

## DEADLY DUMMY

Put a guy in a coffin (a pinebox will do) with his head at the foot and his feet at the head. You then can put a shirt around his calves and knees and stuff it with rags to look like the guy's chest. The collar of the shirt should be around the guy's ankles. Lay a pillow over the guy's feet and just above the shirt collar. Then put a styrofoam head on the pillow with a mask and a wig on it. Cover the guy's thighs, waist, trunk, and head with a blanket. Then as the kids look at the "body," they will think it's just a dummy which won't scare them much. But as they bend over to look at the "dummy's" face, the guy should sit up from the other end and scream in their ears. This works best in a dimly lit room.

## SHRUNKEN HEADS

Hang a sheet in a dark room (like a closet). Cut two holes in the sheet and have two girls stick their heads through it. Tie their hair to the ceiling to give the effect of shrunken heads. Put a little red food coloring under their heads on the sheet and paint some black stitch marks over their lips for effect. A light turned on and off quickly is the best way to show it. That way the kids won't have time to analyze what it really is.

# Thanksgiving

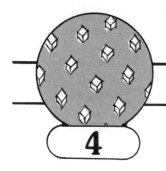

# Thanksgiving

**4**

## Fun and Games

### GOBBLE OFF

This is a crowd breaker that involves the entire group yet turns out to be a hilarious "fall-guy" routine. To begin, send two people out of the room after telling them that they are to be judges in a "Gobble Off" (Turkey Gobbling Contest). After they are out of earshot, take the entire group into confidence and explain that this is a trick to be played on one of the two volunteers (person number one). The object is to get him to "gobble" loudly all by himself after his turn at judging. Go through the entire instructions beforehand, even to the point of rehearsing the "gobbles." The steps are as follows:

First, person number one should come back into the room and stand in the center of a circle. He should be told that he is to judge which member of the group is the loudest "turkey" in the turkey pen after hearing the group gobble three times. He should also be told that the group has chosen a "turkey" to be the loudest one, and that he must try to guess who he is. The group should then gobble once, twice, then a third time, and person number one should be asked who the loudest turkey is. By common consent, whoever he picks will be wrong, and another person will be offered (usually a quieter person) as the "real" loudest turkey. So person number one will lose.

Then person number one should rejoin the group (sits down in the audience). The leader should say that the group must now choose a new "turkey" to be the loudest. After suggesting several (they all decline), the leader should fake that he has a novel idea and should ask person number one to be it—for person number two would never guess him. Others should join in support of the idea, and person number one should be rehearsed several times as the loudest turkey of the group (until he's really gobbling at full strength).

Then comes the trick. When person number two comes into the circle, he should be told to listen for the loudest turkey. The leader must count 1, 2, 3 and everyone must

95

gobble once. He must count again, and everyone must gobble the second time. He must count again and everyone should take a deep breath, but they *must not* gobble. And you will hear a great solo gobble from person number one. You can then award him the Golden Turkey Award.

## THANKSGIVING BINGO

Here's a mixer that works well at Thanksgiving. Simply print up a bingo card like the one illustrated below. Fill in each of the blanks with something that the kids in your group would probably be thankful for. Make some of them very general, like "Someone to love" and others more specific, like "Making the football team." The idea is for everyone to go around the room and to find people who are thankful for particular items. Have them sign their name in the appropriate square. If you get five in a row, up, down, or diagonally, then you are a winner.

| A GOOD SINGING VOICE | MY NEW CAR | MY OWN ROOM | A CLOSE FAMILY | GOOD LOOKS |
|---|---|---|---|---|
| MY 16th BIRTHDAY THIS YEAR | MY STEREO | AN ANSWERED PRAYER | GOOD HEALTH ALL YEAR | MY JOB |
| NO ZITS | SOMEONE WHO LOVES ME | A SUCCESSFUL DIET TO LOSE WEIGHT | A FUN VACATION LAST SUMMER | GETTING TO GO SKIING LAST YEAR |
| MAKING THE TEAM | A FRIEND WHO BECAME A CHRISTIAN | GOOD GRADES | WINNING AN AWARD LAST YEAR | A NEW BABY IN THE FAMILY |
| A BIG BILL PAID OFF LAST YEAR | A BIG PROBLEM RECENTLY SOLVED | FINDING A NEW FRIEND RECENTLY | MY GUITAR-PLAYING ABILITY | NOT FALLING ASLEEP DURING THE SERMON |

Play until everyone has five in a row, and then perhaps each person can share her bingo combination. Encourage each person to not only sign a person's bingo card but to also elaborate on why she is thankful for that particular item. Another rule is that no person may write her name twice on anyone's bingo card; only one square per person. This game can be used with adults as well simply by changing the categories to things like: "My Successful Operation," "My New Granddaughter," "Buying a New Home," and so forth.

## THANKSGIVING SCAVENGER HUNT

A great idea for Thanksgiving is to have a food scavenger hunt in which the food items collected are given to needy families in your area. Meet on a chosen day or evening, divide your group into teams, and give each team a list similar to the one shown here.

| | |
|---|---|
| 10 slices dry white bread | 2 cans of corn or beans |
| 4 pounds yams | 1 pkg. Lucky Whip |
| 3 onions 9" each in circumference | 3 pkgs. Jello |
| 2 yellow apples in A-1 condition | 1 pkg. soft marshmallows |
| 2 red apples | 1 can mandarin oranges |
| 6 California oranges | 1 can fruit cocktail |
| 1 lb. mixed nuts | 1 size 2½ can peaches |
| 5 lbs. red potatoes | 1 can Libby's pumpkin |
| 5 lbs. flour | 1 size 303 can Green Giant peas |
| 1 lb. dark brown sugar | 3 12-oz. cans ginger ale |
| 1 pkg. raisins | 1 can whole cranberry sauce |

The teams should try to bring back as many of the listed items as they possibly can. They should try to get them donated. If they must purchase an item, limit each person to a small amount (like 50¢) which she can spend, and allow only one item to be purchased at any one store. Provide the kids with some kind of identification so that they can show people that they really are with an organization that is donating the food to the needy.

In addition to the items on the list, give additional points for *any* non-perishable grocery items that a team can bring back. At the end of the time limit, each team should meet back at the starting point and display all the food they have gathered for inspection by the "judges," who will determine the winner. It might also be a good idea to have an adding machine on hand to add up the estimated value of the food collected. It will really give the kids a feeling of accomplishment and the satisfaction that their event has been worth a lot to some needy people.

## THANKSGIVING FEAST

This is a banquet or potluck idea for Thanksgiving in which everyone brings a food beginning with the first letter of his or her last name and keeps it a secret. Have tables for eight to ten decorated for the occasion. Each table must eat the "feast" in alphabetical order for the last names of those at their particular table. Between courses have them share blessings, favorite verses of Scripture, plans for the holiday, what they like most about it, and so on.

## TURKEY

This Thanksgiving game is simply a little competition to see which team can do the best job of "decorating a turkey." Divide into three or four groups. Give each group a paper sack full of goodies: an old pair of nylons, a roll of toilet paper, scissors, scotch tape, crepe or tissue paper, newspaper, or anything else you might be able to think of that will contribute to making a person look like a turkey. Set a time limit. You should explain to the kids what they are to do, then divide the room up. Have each group select one person to be the "turkey." Give them three or four minutes to do the decorating and then have the whole group be judges and decide the winner by applause.

## TURKEY OF THE YEAR

This could be used as a fund-raiser to provide food or clothing for needy families at Thanksgiving. Have a "Turkey of the Year" contest at your church in which you "nominate" several key people by posting their photos over some canning jars which have slits in the top for money to be inserted. The congregation can vote for their favorite "turkey" by contributing money into the appropriate jar. Since you will be able to see the money, it will keep the competition close. You can have each nominee give a sample "gobble" in church or give a campaign speech (for the other nominees) to add to the fun. At the end, award a Turkey Trophy and announce the winning amount (as well as the total that was raised).

## TURKEY TEST

To get a few groans (or gobbles) from your kids, give them this little Thanksgiving quiz:

1. What part of the turkey is like a story?
2. Why is a glutton like a turkey?
3. What part of a turkey is like part of a sentence?
4. What part of the turkey does the farmer watch most anxiously?
5. What part of the turkey do you keep on the dressing table?
6. What part of the turkey makes the most noise?
7. What are the turkey's last clothes?

ANSWERS:

1. The tail
2. He gobbles
3. The claws
4. The crop
5. The comb
6. The drumstick
7. His dressing

## TURKEY SHOOT

Draw up two large turkeys (on paper) which can be covered with a sheet of glass. The guns for the turkey shoot should be toy suction-cup dart guns that shoot twenty feet or so. The paper turkeys should be divided up into eight sections with each section naming a particular "action" that has to be performed. There should be two teams, and each team should have a gun. Each team must elect a "turkey" who will stand in front of the entire group. Team A shoots at their paper turkey, and whatever "action" they hit, Team B's "turkey" must do, and vice versa. Play until everyone has had a chance to shoot. It's good for a lot of laughs. Some sample "actions" can include: gobble like a turkey, flap wings, say "I'm a turkey" five times, do five pushups, hop around the team on one foot, do five deep knee bends, get a pie in the face, etc.

## TURKEY SHOOT II

This game can be played with any size group from six to sixty. The leader should have everyone assemble in one large circle, with all the participants facing in the same direction. Each one in the circle should then put his hand on the shoulder of the person ahead of him. Several leaders (or young people), depending on the size of the group, should stand at various spots within the circle facing those in the circle and should be armed with loaded squirt guns. At a given signal, the leader should have the whole group rotate in a circle while music is being played (or until a whistle is blown). When the music stops, the person immediately in front of each of the armed leaders is shot with the squirt gun just like a "sitting turkey." The ones who have been shot must leave the game. The circle then closes up and the music begins again. The circle again moves around until the music stops and the "turkeys" are shot. This procedure continues until only one person is left. The last one to stay in the game is declared the winner. (As more and more participants leave the game the leader might want to decrease the number of shooters.) This game is exciting and the tension runs high.

# Creative Communication

## COUNTING BIBLICAL BLESSINGS

Print up a sheet with the following Scripture verses on it, and ask the group to write after each verse what the various writers or biblical characters were thankful for.

| | |
|---|---|
| Psalm 30:4–5 | 1 Corinthians 15:55–57 |
| Psalm 97:10–12 | 2 Corinthians 2:14 |
| 1 Chronicles 29:6–13 | 2 Corinthians 9:15 |
| Daniel 2:23 | Philippians 1:3–5 |
| Acts 27:34–35 | 2 Thessalonians 1:2–3 |
| Romans 1:8 | 1 Timothy 4:3–5 |
| Romans 6:17–18 | Revelation 11:16–17 |

After the group has done this, have them choose one or two items from the list for which they are also thankful. They can then share these with each other and have a time of thanking God for them through group prayer.

## IN EVERYTHING, GIVE THANKS

For a special program on giving thanks to God for everything, invite a Christian to come to your group meeting who is obviously handicapped in some way (blind, confined to a wheelchair, etc.). Then interview him or her before the group, asking questions similar to these:

1. Many Christians believe that we should thank God for our troubles or for bad things that happen. How do you feel about this?

2. What have you found to be thankful for in the midst of your own suffering with your handicap?

3. What is the best thing that God has done for you? What is the thing for which you are most thankful?

4. What is the hardest thing that you have found to give thanks to God for? Are there things that you have found you cannot really thank God for?

After the interview, give the group some time to question your guest, then give each person in the group the following questions. Ask them to work through these on their own.

1. Are there things in my life that I have found difficult to thank God for? Can I thank Him now?
2. Complete this sentence: When someone thanks me for something, I feel . . .
3. When was the last time that you thanked someone for something?
4. Make a list of some things that you need to thank God for.
5. Make a list of people who you need to thank for something.

This exercise can then be followed up with some small group sharing or by a time of commitment, centered on our need to be more grateful for the many things we take for granted in life or don't feel very thankful for.

## MY REASONS FOR THANKSGIVING

Give each person a pencil and paper. On the paper should be printed the words: MY REASONS FOR THANKSGIVING. If you can't print it ahead of time, have each person write it across the top of the page. Then have each person write down as many things as he can think of that he is thankful for—using only the letters in the statement at the top of the page. No letter may be used more times than it appears in the statement. Set a time limit of around ten minutes. It makes a fun game but also a good discussion starter on the topic of giving thanks.

## THANKSGIVING EXCHANGE

This is a good discussion starter for Thanksgiving or for any time you want to teach a lesson on gratitude. It works best with a group that knows each other fairly well. Begin by having each person share one or two things that she is thankful for. These will usually be the kind of things that are most obvious to her.

Then have each person write his or her name on the top of a sheet of paper. Collect the sheets and redistribute them so that everyone has a sheet with someone else's name on it. Now have each person write on that sheet what she would be thankful for if she were the person whose name is on that sheet. She can list as many things as she wants. Following this, pass the sheets back to the person whose name is on each sheet and discuss the following questions:

1. What things are written on your sheet that you haven't thanked God for lately?
2. What things are written on your sheet that you have never even thought about thanking God for?
3. Is anything written on your sheet that you disagree with or that you don't think you should be thankful for?

This exercise helps young people realize that they often take for granted many things that they should be thankful for.

## THANKSGIVING GRAFFITI

Have some of your young people hang up a large blank sheet of paper in a well-traveled area in your church. The pastor can announce that after the service people are invited to write, print, or draw something that represents what they are thankful for. The young people should be ready with felt-tip pens, crayons, water colors, etc. for people to use. If this is done early in November, the resulting graffiti can be displayed in a prominent place to remind people of how much we do have to be thankful for.

## THE THANKFUL LEPER

Use this exercise as a way to point kids toward recognizing the need for expressing thanks to God rather than constantly bombarding Him with requests. Give each person a mimeographed copy of Luke 17:11–19, the account of Jesus healing the ten lepers. A modern translation of the passage is the most effective. Another sheet with the following questions and instructions should then be handed to each person.

> Read carefully the account of Jesus healing the ten lepers. As you read, attempt to identify with the feelings of the lepers who did not return to thank Jesus, with the leper who did, and with Jesus in this situation. Then answer the following questions:
>
> 1. How do you think Christ felt when only one individual out of ten returned to give thanks?
> 2. Describe what you think the grateful leper must have felt and thought during his healing encounter with Christ.
> 3. What excuses can you think of for the nine healed lepers who did not return to give thanks to Christ?
>
> Now attempt to apply this passage of Scripture to your life by reacting to the following:
>
> 1. With whom in this story do you most identify, the nine who did not return or the one who came back?
> 2. What excuses do you usually think of for not thanking Christ for what He has done in your life?
> 3. What was the last thing Christ did for you or provided for you that you wish to thank Him for?
> 4. Using the paper and colors provided for you, construct a colorful thank you card addressed to Christ. The outside of the card should express through symbolic colors and expressive symbols the event or object for which you are thankful. In the inside of the card, write a short letter, poem, or prayer that expresses your thankfulness.

After completing this assignment, divide the kids into small groups to share their answers and explain the meanings of the cards they made. Close the meeting with prayer, emphasizing thanksgiving.

# Christmas

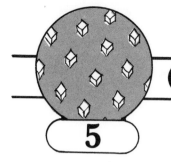

# Christmas

## 5

## Fun and Games

### ALL I WANT FOR CHRISTMAS . . .

This is a good game for groups of around twenty people. The group should be seated in a circle. The first person should complete the sentence, "All I want for Christmas is . . ." After naming what he wants for Christmas, the next person in the circle must repeat what the first person said and add what he wants for Christmas. This should continue all the way around the circle, with the list getting longer and longer. The object is simply to name each item in order without making a mistake when it is your turn; obviously, it's harder when you are one of the last few people. If you miss, you are out; the rest keep going around the circle until only one person is left. That person is the winner.

### BLIZZARD BLAST

Here's a special event or party idea that works great at Christmas, especially if you live in an area where the climate is warm during the winter. The theme is "snow" or "ice" and you play games that incorporate that theme. Teams can have names like "The Icicles," "The Snowdrifts," "The Snowflakes," and so on. Here are a few sample games that you can play:

1. *Snowball Fight:* Teams wad up stacks of newspaper into "snowballs" and throw them into the other team's "territory." The team with the least amount of snow in their territory at the end of the game is the winner.
2. *Ice Melting Contest:* Each team gets a block of ice and must try to melt it using only their hands (rubbing it). The ice is weighed at the beginning of the game and again after the game is over. The ice block that has lost the most weight wins. The game can go for about ten to fifteen minutes.
3. *Mining for Marbles:* Team members try to find marbles hidden in a large pan of crushed ice . . . using only their toes.
4. *Snowflake Contest:* Kids compete to see who can cut the best "snowflake" out of newspaper.

5. *Ski Relay:* Make skis (old shoes nailed to strips of wood) and have the kids put them on and race in them. You can also do this with snowshoes.
6. *Snowman Feed:* Hold a pie-eating contest, using lots of whipped cream. No hands are allowed.

If you live somewhere where you can go to the snow (like up in the mountains) and bring back a big truckload of snow for this event, you can create some "authentic" snow games. Refreshments can include varieties of ice cream, snow cones, iced tea, and so on. Use your own creativity and this event can be a lot of fun.

## CAROLING COMPETITION

Divide into two teams. Each team should have a leader who can lead his or her team in some Christmas carols. The game is played like the old game of "Musical Mother Goose." Team #1 begins by singing one verse of a Christmas song or carol as fast as they can. As soon as they finish their verse, Team #2 must begin another carol and sing it. After they have finished their verse, it goes back to Team #1 who must start singing another new song, and so on. The first team that fails to start singing a new Christmas song or carol (or to complete singing a verse) loses the game. Teams are allowed five seconds after the conclusion of the other team's song to get started. It should keep going back and forth until one team blows it. It's an exciting way to sing a lot of Christmas songs.

## CAROLING TREASURE HUNT

Here's a great way to go Christmas caroling this year. Divide into "Caroling Groups" of between six and ten people and make a treasure hunt out of it. Each group should be given a first "clue" which (when figured out) gives the location of the first place where they are to sing Christmas carols. It could be at someone's home, at a rest home, at a shopping center, or anywhere you choose. The group must go there and sing at least four Christmas carols (chosen ahead of time) all the way through, ending with "We Wish You a Merry Christmas." They must pick up the next clue at that location (or they might have the next clue already with them in a sealed envelope) and then head for the next location, and so on. It could be worked out so that none of the caroling groups duplicate locations, or some locations could get lots of carolers in one night. The last destination could be the location of a Christmas party with refreshments and games.

## CHRISTMAS BELL TRADE

Here's a fairly tame little mixer that works well at Christmas parties and socials. Give each person a small paper bell made out of red construction paper. It should be small enough so that it can be concealed in a clenched fist. One person should be given a gold bell instead of a red one. When the game begins, the kids should mill around the room with both fists clenched, hiding the bells. One person may then go up to another and say, "Merry Christmas" (or anything you choose as a "password"). On doing so, the other person must hold out his fists, and the person who said Merry

Christmas must try to guess which hand holds the bell. If he or she is correct, the two players must trade bells. Players are not allowed to trade bells with the same person twice in a row. They may try to trade with that person only after they have traded with someone else first. At the end of the time limit (usually five minutes is long enough), the game should stop and the person who is holding the gold bell is the winner.

## CHRISTMAS CAROL CHARADES

Divide into two teams (or more if you have a larger group). Give each team a pad of large-size drawing paper and a marking pen. Each team should be stationed in a different part of the room. You, as leader, will stand in the middle of the room at an equal distance from all the teams. You should have in your hand a stack of 3 x 5 cards with names of Christmas songs and carols on them.

Each team must be seated, and they should pick someone from their group to go first. That person should come to you and should be shown the name of the first song or carol. (Each team gets the same one at the same time.) Then when you say "go," the person who got the carol must run back to their team, pick up the drawing paper and pen, and try to draw a picture that will help his or her team to guess the name of the carol. Once they have correctly guessed it, they must sing a few lines of it. The first team to do this is the winner of that round.

Another person from the team should be selected, a new carol should be given, and the game should continue. The people who are doing the drawing may not talk, nor may they draw letters or words. They may draw only pictures. They may say yes or no as people are guessing, but that's all.

## CHRISTMAS CAROL PUZZLE

Take an old book of Christmas carols and cut up the old favorites into jig-saw puzzles. Make sure each piece has a few key words or if the group is more musically inclined, a few key notes. Pass out the pieces to the group. Have them find the other members of their sub-group by putting their Christmas carol puzzle together. When the groups are established, have them sing their song for the others.

## CHRISTMAS CAROL TAG

Divide the group into two teams. The object of this simple game is for each team to try to eliminate members of the opposing team by tagging them. The only time a person is safe and cannot be tagged is while singing a Christmas carol or song. A person cannot, however, sing the same verse of the same song more than once. The last team to have surviving members is the winner.

## CHRISTMAS CAROLS TO SHOP BY

The following "carols" are great fun to sing during the holiday season. The message of each rings through loud and clear. They were written by Mike Royko and appeared originally in the *Chicago Daily News* and are reprinted here with permission.

Tune: DECK THE HALLS

Deck the streets with phony holly,
Fa-la-la-la-la-la-la-la-la!
Christmas makes the merchants jolly,
Fa-la-la-la-la-la-la-la-la!
Windows full of gifts to please us,
Fa-la-la-la-la-la-la-la-la!
Happy Birthday, little Jesus,
Fa-la-la-la-la-la-la-la-la!

Tune: O LITTLE TOWN OF
BETHLEHEM

O, little town on Christmas Eve
How busy art thou tonight!
Thy stores won't close 'til 10 o'clock,
Thy streets are thronged and bright.
The clerks are tired and cranky,
The merchandise is junk.
The little dears are all in tears,
And Santa Claus is drunk.

Tune: JINGLE BELLS

Dashing through the streets,
Snarling as you go;
If someone's in your way,
Shove the so-and so.
Whizzing through the doors,
Charging down the aisles,
All the Christmas faces wreathed
In tense and nervous smiles.

(Chorus) Oh, buy our stuff!
Buy our stuff!
Empty out your purse!
Christmas is a spending time
That steadily grows worse.
Oh, we have got . . . lovely gifts
For each Him and Her.
If we're out of frankincense,
Buy our dandy myrrh!

Tune: SANTA CLAUS IS COMING TO
TOWN

Y'better not mope, Y'better not frown,
Y'better not keep expenditures down,
Santa Claus is coming to town.
Y'better not scrimp, Y'better not save,
Ya gotta give more than the other guy
   gave,
Santa Claus is coming to town.

So load up all your charge accounts
And let the payments wait
And send expensive Christmas cards
To people that you hate, hate, hate!

Y'better not whine, Y'better not cry,
Everything's fine just as long as you
   buy;
Santa Claus is coming to town.

Tune: GOOD KING WENCESLAUS

Good King Wenceslaus went out,
Ere the Feast of Stephen:
Merchandise lay all about,
Priced beyond believin'.
"Gee," said Good King Wenceslaus,
"Such expensive presents!
Isn't it a lucky thing
I can tax the pea-ea-sants?"

Tune: O COME, ALL YE FAITHFUL

O come all you buyers,
How 'bout some radial tires?
Or maybe you want to give
A mink to your love.
Come sign at the bottom,
You don't need no cash, chum;
O come and let us sell you,
O come and let us dun you,
O come and let us sue you-hoo,
Welcome aboard!

## CHRISTMAS CONFUSION

For this holiday mixer, give everyone in your group a copy of the game sheet below. Read over the instructions to the group to make sure they understand them. The object is to finish all the instructions correctly before anyone else. The first one finished could receive a prize of some kind. The instructions can be completed in any order.

# Christmas Confusion

1. Get five autographs on the back of this sheet (first, middle, last names).

2. Find three other people and sing together, "We Wish You a Merry Christmas" as loudly as you can. Then initial each other's papers here. _____
_____ _____

3. Tell someone the names of three of Santa's reindeer. Then have that person initial here. _____

4. You play Santa Claus. Find someone of the opposite sex, sit him or her on your lap, and ask what he or she wants for Christmas. Then have him or her initial here. _____

5. Pick the ornament on the Christmas tree which you like the best. Find someone else and give them a 15-second speech on why you like that particular ornament. Then have that person initial here. _____

6. You are Ebenezer Scrooge. Find someone and ask them to wish you a Merry Christmas. When they do, say, "Bah, Humbug," ten times while jumping up and down. Then have that person initial here. _____

7. Leapfrog over someone wearing red or green. Then have them initial here.
_____

8. Find someone of the opposite sex and have them whistle one verse of "Away In A Manger" to you. Then have that person initial here. _____

## CHRISTMAS COSTUME PARTY

A unique touch for a great Christmas Party would be to have everyone come dressed as a character or thing that is associated with Christmas or the Christmas story. Possibilities might include any of the biblical characters like Mary and Joseph, the wise men, the innkeeper, the shepherds, Herod, and so forth. Or someone could dress like one of the animals, the star of Bethlehem, an angel—the list could go on and on. It could also be expanded to include non-biblical Christmas characters and things like Santa, Mrs. Santa, Rudolph, Frosty the Snowman, a Christmas package, a toy soldier, a doll, or even a Christmas tree.

To add more meaning to this, have a time at the conclusion of the party for each person to share what Christmas means to him, from the perspective of the person or thing he is dressed as.

## CHRISTMAS FAMILY FEUD

This game is based on the TV game, "Family Feud," but with a Christmas flavor. You don't need all the fancy buzzers and scoreboards that are used on TV. The game does require a little advance preparation, however.

First, prepare a short "survey" using the questions below. Give the survey to one of your adult Sunday school classes or to the entire church if you can. Have them write in anything that will correctly answer each question. After this has been done, take all the completed surveys and tally up the results. Find out the top five answers for each question.

After you have the results, the game will be ready for the youth group. Divide into teams (as on "Family Feud"). Flip a coin to determine which team goes first. The first question should then be read to that team. The team must decide on an answer and tell you what it is. If they choose the #1 answer (according to the survey results) they get 50 points. If they choose the #2 answer, they get 40 points, and if they get the #3 answer, they get 30 points, and so on. Each team gets one guess at a time, and then the other team gets a try. In other words, the first team might guess the #2 answer on their first try, which would allow the other team a chance to guess the #1 answer and collect the 50 points. Any guess which isn't one of the top five answers (a "strike" on the TV version) can be a loss of ten points. If all the points available on one question have not been won by either team after five guesses by each team, then go on to the next question. It's a lot of fun with a lot of tension.

Here are some sample questions for your "survey":

1. Name something you hang on a Christmas tree.
2. Name a Christmas carol.
3. Name a word on a Christmas card other than "Merry" or "Christmas."
4. Name one of Santa's reindeer.
5. A role someone might play in a Christmas pageant.
6. The color of a Christmas tree light.
7. The number of days you leave your tree up after Christmas.
8. A book of the Bible that tells about Christ's birth.
9. How old were you when you found out there was no such thing as Santa Claus?
10. Name a Christmas decoration, other than a tree.
11. Name something associated with Santa Claus.
12. Name something people usually do on Christmas day.
13. Name a food or beverage that is popular at Christmas.
14. The shape of a typical Christmas cookie.
15. How many weeks before Christmas should Christmas cards be put in the mail?

## CHRISTMAS GIFT GUESSING

By the time that most of us are grown, we have become experts at shaking and feeling Christmas packages to find out what is inside them. So the object of this game is to test that skill and allow kids to shake and feel for prizes. Wrap up about ten packages and line them up in a row. Number them from 1 to 10 and give each person a piece of paper and pencil. The idea is to shake and feel each package and then guess what is in each. Whoever comes the closest to guessing all ten wins her choice of the ten gifts, and so on down the line (with the tenth most accurate guess getting the last gift in order of preference). You might help the guessing along by giving the kids a list of "possible" gifts that might be in the packages. For example, if you have ten gifts, you might give them twenty answers with the correct ones included, and they must match them up with the numbers on the packages.

## CHRISTMAS GROUP DRAMATICS

Here's an audience participation activity that can be a lot of fun. Divide the audience into six groups. Each group should be given a word and a corresponding response. Then the following poem should be read (see below). Every time a group's word is mentioned, they must respond with the correct phrase.

Santa—"Ho, Ho, Ho"
Reindeer—"Clippity Clop"
Rudolph—"Beep, Beep" (While pinching nose)
Bells—"Jingle, Jingle"
Snow—"Br-r-r-r"
Sleigh—"Wheeeeeee!"

One time long ago in a fake little town
A happening happened and the story's told 'round
How a reindeer named Rudolph was of no help to Santa
Delivering presents in this town near Atlanta.

The sleigh owned by Santa was loaded with presents
By the elves and the reindeer and a large group of peasants.
The reindeer were harnessed with bells on their toes,
But Rudolph must stay home (because of his nose).

Santa, the reindeer and the sleigh were all ready
To deliver the presents when a problem quite heady
Developed. It stopped them, they just couldn't go.
The problem, you see, was a large storm of snow.

The snow came so hard that Santa couldn't see.
The reindeer wouldn't know where to pull the sleigh (whee).
The reindeer, bells jingling, and Santa made tracks
Through the snow to see Rudolph, a question to ask.

Rudolph, said Santa and the reindeer in unison,
If this snow stops us this year our act is for sure done.
We've a sleigh full of presents to deliver tonight,
And the snow is so heavy, we have little sight.

Will you and your nose guide the reindeer to housetops
So that Santa with presents can make all of his stops?
Rudolph yawned and looked out at the wind driven snow
And said, "Santa and reindeer, I just cannot go."

The sleigh is too heavy with presents delightful,
But if you ask me, the job seems a might dull.
Besides, all this snow and your bells out of tune,
The cold is too much. Ask again come next June.

111

# CHRISTMAS I.Q. TEST

This Christmas give the following "quiz" to your youth to determine how much they *really* know about the Bible's most popular story. The results will undoubtedly be very embarrassing, but they will also lead to a better understanding of the events surrounding Christ's birth.

*Instructions:*

Read and answer each question in the order it appears. When choices are given, read them carefully and select the best one. Put a "T" or an "F" in the blank on all True or False questions. Guessing is permitted, cheating is not.

_____ 1. As long as Christmas has been celebrated, it has been on December 25. *(True or False)*

_____ 2. Joseph was from:
    A. Bethlehem          D. Egypt
    B. Jerusalem          E. Minnesota
    C. Nazareth          F. None of the above

_____ 3. How did Mary and Joseph travel to Bethlehem?
    A. Camel          E. Joseph walked, Mary rode
    B. Donkey            a donkey
    C. Walked          F. Who knows?
    D. Volkswagen

_____ 4. Mary and Joseph were married when Mary became pregnant. *(True or False)*

_____ 5. Mary and Joseph were married when Jesus was born. *(True or False)*

_____ 6. Mary was a virgin when she delivered Jesus. *(True or False)*

_____ 7. What did the innkeeper tell Mary and Joseph?
    A. "There is no room in the inn."    D. Both A and B
    B. "I have a stable you can use."    E. None of the above
    C. "Come back after the
        Christmas rush and I should
        have some vacancies."

_____ 8. Jesus was delivered in a:
    A. Stable          D. Barn
    B. Manger          E. Unknown
    C. Cave

_____ 9. A "manger" is a:
    A. Stable for domestic animals    C. Feeding trough
    B. Wooden hay storage bin      D. Barn

_____ 10. Which animals does the Bible say were present at Jesus' birth?
    A. Cows, sheep, goats      D. Miscellaneous barnyard
    B. Cows, donkeys, sheep         animals
    C. Sheep and goats only      E. Lions, tigers, elephants
                             F. None of the above

_____ 11. Who saw the "star in the east"?
  A. Shepherds                D. Both A and C
  B. Mary and Joseph          E. None of the above
  C. Three Kings

_____ 12. How many angels spoke to the shepherds?
  A. One                      C. A "Multitude"
  B. Three                    D. None of the above

_____ 13. What "sign" did the angels tell the shepherds to look for?
  A. "This way to baby Jesus" D. A house with a Christmas tree
  B. A star over Bethlehem    E. A baby in a stable
  C. A baby that doesn't cry  F. None of the above

_____ 14. What did the angels sing?
  A. "Joy to the World, the Lord Is    D. "Glory to God in the highest,
     Come"                                etc."
  B. "Alleluia"               E. "Glory to the Newborn King"
  C. "Unto us a child is born, unto    F. "My Sweet Lord"
     us a son is given"

_____ 15. What is a "Heavenly Host"?
  A. The angel at the gate of D. An angel choir
     heaven                   E. An angel army
  B. The angel who invites people    F. None of the above
     to heaven
  C. The angel who serves refresh-
     ments in heaven

_____ 16. There was snow that first Christmas:
  A. Only in Bethlehem        D. Somewhere in Israel.
  B. All over Israel          E. Mary and Joseph only
  C. Nowhere in Israel           "dreamed" of a white
                                 Christmas

_____ 17. The baby Jesus cried:
  A. When the doctor slapped Him    C. Just like other babies cry
     on His behind            D. He never cried
  B. When the little drummer boy
     started banging on his drum

_____ 18. What is "frankincense"?
  A. A precious metal         D. An Eastern monster story
  B. A precious fabric        E. None of the above
  C. A precious perfume

_____ 19. What is "myrrh"?
  A. An easily shaped metal   C. A drink
  B. A spice used for burying D. After-shave lotion
     people                   E. None of the above

_____ 20. How many wise men came to see Jesus?
  (Write in the correct number.)

113

_____ 21. What does "wise men" refer to?
  A. Men of the educated class
  B. They were Eastern kings
  C. They were astrologers
  D. They were smart enough to follow the star
  E. They were "sages"

_____ 22. The wise men found Jesus in a:
  A. Manger
  B. Stable
  C. House
  D. Holiday Inn
  E. Good Mood

_____ 23. The wise men stopped in Jerusalem:
  A. To inform Herod about Jesus
  B. To find out where Jesus was
  C. To ask about the star that they saw
  D. For gas
  E. To buy presents for Jesus

_____ 24. Where do we find the Christmas story in order to check up on all these ridiculous questions?
  A. Matthew
  B. Mark
  C. Luke
  D. John
  E. All of the above
  F. Only A and B
  G. Only A and C
  H. Only A, B, and C
  I. Only X, Y, and Z
  F. Aesops Fables

_____ 25. When Joseph and Mary found out that Mary was pregnant with Jesus, what happened?
  A. They got married
  B. Joseph wanted to break the engagement
  C. Mary left town for three months.
  D. An angel told them to go to Bethlehem
  E. Both A and D
  F. Both B and C

_____ 26. Who told Mary and Joseph to go to Bethlehem?
  A. The angel
  B. Mary's mother
  C. Herod
  D. Caesar Augustus
  E. Alexander the Great
  F. No one told them to

_____ 27. Joseph took the baby Jesus to Egypt:
  A. To show Him the pyramids
  B. To teach Him the wisdom of the pharaohs
  C. To put Him in a basket in the reeds by the river
  D. Because he dreamed about it
  E. To be taxed
  F. Joseph did not take Jesus to Egypt
  G. None of the above

_____ 28. I think that this test was:
  A. Super
  B. Great
  C. Fantastic
  D. All of the above

**ANSWERS:**

1. False. Not until the 4th century did it settle on the 25th. Other dates were accepted before then.
2. A. See Luke 2:3–4.

114

3. F. The Bible doesn't say.
4. False. See Matthew 1:18.
5. False. See Luke 2:5.
6. True. See Matthew 1:25.
7. E. No word about the innkeeper. See Luke 2:7.
8. E. No word about it. See Luke 2:7.
9. C.
10. F. The Bible doesn't specify.
11. E. The *wise men* did (they were not kings). See Matthew 2:2.
12. A. See Luke 2:9.
13. F. See Luke 2:12.
14. D. See Luke 2:14.
15. E. Definition is an "army." See *Living Bible* also.
16. D. Mt. Hermon is snow covered.
17. C. We have no reason to believe He wouldn't.
18. C. By definition.
19. B. See John 19:39 or a dictionary.
20. No one knows. See Matthew 2:1.
21. C. See most any commentary. They were astrologers or "star gazers."
22. C. See Matthew 2:11.
23. B. See Matthew 2:1–2.
24. G. Mark begins with John the Baptist, John with "the word."
25. F. See Matthew 1:19, Luke 1:39, 56.
26. D. See Luke 2:1, 4.
27. D. See Matthew 2:13.
28. D, of course.

## CHRISTMAS IN OTHER LANDS

If you are tired of the "same old thing" every Christmas for parties and other special events, try this. Hold a party and have everyone bring a food dish from another country. For example:

| | |
|---|---|
| Mexican: | tacos, enchiladas, etc. |
| Chinese: | egg rolls, chop suey |
| Italian: | spaghetti, lasagna, pizza |
| French: | crepes, yule log |
| Danish: | pastries |
| England: | wassail, tea, fish and chips |

Everyone should dress in a costume from another country (if possible), and various people should be assigned to share the different ways that Christmas is celebrated in foreign cultures. Your public library can be helpful for getting information and finding games that are used in other countries. These customs can then be compared to those in the U.S.A. This can be a great learning experience as well as a lot of fun.

## CHRISTMAS IN JULY

This really goes over because it's so crazy. Hold a full-fledged Christmas Party in July or August (or anytime during the summer) complete with Christmas decorations,

Christmas carols, and all the rest. If it is done properly, a real Christmas-time spirit can be created. Have everyone bring a gift to exchange. Surprisingly enough, the Christmas story makes a deeper impact at this time of the year when it is separated from all the hustle and bustle of the usual holiday season.

**CHRISTMAS-GRAMS**

Here's a creative way for your youth group to raise money for their favorite Christmas-time project (such as taking a group of orphans Christmas shopping or hosting a party for the crippled children's ward at the hospital). Sell *Christmas-Grams*. First plan a get-together to make them. Have on hand plenty of red and green net (the material can be purchased from any fabric shop and is extra wide and inexpensive), red and green yarn, loads of individual wrapped candies, and red and green construction paper. Decide on a shape for a cut-out: a star, a Christmas tree, or a Christmas bell. Cut the construction paper into the decided shape, approximately three inches by three inches. This will be used for people to write their messages on. Cut the net into small squares and place two or three pieces of candy inside the net. Tie a piece of yarn around the net. Use a hole puncher to make a hole in the construction cut-out and run the yarn through it to attach to the net-wrapped candies. Tie the yarn in a bow. Now you have a "Christmas-Gram."

Decide on a place in the church to set up a Christmas-Gram booth. Advertise through your church paper and through posters throughout the church. Invite people to buy a Christmas-Gram, write a message on one side of the construction paper cut-out, and write the name of the person to whom it is to be delivered on the other side. For a determined amount, the youth can furnish the Christmas-Gram and deliver it.

## CHRISTMAS MAD LIBS

Below are three "Mad Libs" that are great at Christmas time. Simply ask the group to furnish you with some words that will help you to finish these "stories." Don't let the group know what the stories are until they have given you the words to fill in the blanks. Ask the group for the wildest words they can think of (within reason, of course). For example, if you ask for a noun, the group should come up with some really crazy "things" like: bellybutton, outhouse, diaper, cigarette butt, manhole cover, etc. Be selective as the words are shouted out by the group, pick the best ones, and write them in. Then read the completed story back to the group. Most of the time it will be really funny.

### A CHRISTMAS POEM

'Twas the _____ before Christmas and all through the _____ ,
        (noun)                                              (noun)
Not a creature was stirring, not even a _____ .
                                    (noun)
The _____ were hung by the _____ with care,
    (plural noun)                     (noun)
In hopes that _____ would soon be _____ .
         (person in the room)                (adv.)
The _____ were nestled all snug in their _____ ,
    (plural noun)                      (plural noun)
While visions of _____ danced in their _____ .
          (plural noun)             (plural noun)
And Mom in her _____ and I in my _____ ,
         (noun)                  (noun)
Had just settled down for a _____ winter's _____ .
              (adj.)              (noun)
When out on the _____ there arose such a clatter,
           (noun)
I _____-ed from my _____ to see what was the matter.
  (verb)             (noun)
Away to the _____ , I _____-ed like a flash,
       (noun)          (verb)
Tore open the _____ and threw up the sash.
        (noun)
When what to my wondering _____ should appear,
               (part of body)
But a _____ sleigh and eight _____ reindeer.
    (adj.)             (adj.)
With a little old driver, so lively and _____ ,
                    (adj.)
I knew in a moment it must be _____ .
                (person in the room)
More rapid than _____ , the _____ they came,
        (noun)       (noun)
And he _____-ed and _____-ed and called them by name:
    (verb)          (verb)

117

On _____ and _____ . On _____ and _____ .
　　　(name)　　　　　　(name)　　　　　　　(name)　　　　　　(name)

On _____ and _____ and _____ and _____ .
　　　(name)　　　　　　(name)　　　　　　(name)　　　　　　(name)

But I heard him _____ as he drove out of sight,
　　　　　　　　　　　　(verb)

"_____ Christmas to all and to all a good _____ !"
　　(Adj.)　　　　　　　　　　　　　　　　　　　　　　　(noun)

## LETTER TO SANTA

Dear Santa,

How are you? I am _____ . Do you remember me? I am the little _____
　　　　　　　　　　　(adj.)　　　　　　　　　　　　　　　　　　　　　　　　(noun)

who sat on your _____ at the Broadway Dept. Store. I was wearing
　　　　　　　　　(part of body)

_____ pants and a _____ shirt. You probably can remember me
　(color)　　　　　　　　　　　　(adj.)

best by my _____ nose, my _____ eyes, and my face that is
　　　　　　　(adj.)　　　　　　　　　　(adj.)

completely covered with _____ .
　　　　　　　　　　　　(noun)

Santa, for Christmas, I would like an electric _____ , a real "Tommy
　　　　　　　　　　　　　　　　　　　　　　　　　　(noun)

_____" gun, a transistor _____ , and a new baby _____ .
　(noun)　　　　　　　　　　　　　(noun)　　　　　　　　　　　　　(noun)

Santa, if you will bring me all these things, I promise to be a good little _____ ,
　　　　　　　　　　　　　　　　　　　　　　　　　　　　　　　　　　　　(noun)

and to always eat my _____ _____ , and to always clean
　　　　　　　　　　　　(adj.)　　　　　　　(noun)

my _____ .
　　(noun)

Merry Christmas and A Happy New _____ .
　　　　　　　　　　　　　　　　　　(noun)

Your friend, _____
　　　　　　　　　　(person in the room)

## RUDOLPH, THE RED-NOSED REINDEER
### (Sing this one to the group)

Rudolph the _____-nosed _____
                    (adj.)                    (noun)

Had a very _____ nose.
                  (adj.)

And if you ever _____ it,
                      (verb)

You would really say it glows.

All of the other _____
                        (noun)

Used to _____ and call him _____
              (verb)                              (noun)

They never let _____ Rudolph
                      (adj.)

_____ in any _____ games.
      (Verb)                    (adj.)

Then one _____ Christmas Eve,
                (adj.)

Santa _____ to say,
            (verb)

"Rudolph, with your _____ so _____
                        (part of body)        (adj.)

Won't you _____ my _____ tonight?"
                (verb)                (noun)

Then how the reindeer _____-ed him
                            (verb)

As they _____-ed out with _____ ,
              (verb)                          (noun)

"Rudolph, the _____-nosed reindeer,
                    (adj.)

You'll go down in _____ ."
                        (noun)

## CHRISTMAS SYNONYMS

Here's a fun "quiz" that you can use with any age group around Christmas. Print up enough copies for everyone and have the group "translate" each of the twenty-two statements listed back into recognizable English. Each one is a common Christmas saying or song.

1. Move hitherward the entire assembly of those who are loyal in their belief.
2. Listen, the celestial messengers produce harmonious sounds.
3. Nocturnal timespan of unbroken quietness.
4. An emotion excited by the acquisition or expectation of good given to the terrestrial sphere.
5. Embellish the interior passageways.
6. Exalted heavenly beings to whom hearkened.
7. Twelve o'clock on a clement night witnessed its arrival.
8. The Christmas preceding all others.
9. Small municipality in Judea southeast of Jerusalem.
10. Diminutive masculine master of skin-covered percussionistic cylinders.
11. Omnipotent supreme being who elicits respite to ecstatic distinguished males.
12. Tranquility upon the terrestrial sphere.
13. Obese personification fabricated of compressed mounds of minute crystals.
14. Expectation of arrival to populated area by mythical, masculine perennial gift-giver.

15. Natal celebration devoid of color.
16. In awe of the nocturnal time span characterized by religiosity.
17. Geographic state of fantasy during the season of mother nature's dormancy.
18. The first person nominative plural of a triumvirate of far eastern heads of state.
19. Tintinnabulation of vacillating pendulums in inverted, metallic, resonant cups.
20. In a distant location the existence of an improvised unit of newborn children's slumber furniture.
21. Proceed forth declaring upon a specific geological alpine formation.
22. Jovial yuletide desired for the second person singular or plural by us.

The answers:

1. O Come, All Ye Faithful
2. Hark, the Herald Angels Sing
3. Silent Night
4. Joy to the World
5. Deck the Halls
6. Angels We Have Heard on High
7. It Came Upon a Midnight Clear
8. The First Noel
9. O Little Town of Bethlehem
10. Little Drummer Boy
11. God Rest Ye Merry, Gentlemen
12. Peace on Earth
13. Frosty the Snowman
14. Santa Claus Is Coming to Town
15. White Christmas
16. O Holy Night
17. Winter Wonderland
18. We Three Kings of Orient Are
19. Jingle Bells
20. Away in a Manger
21. Go Tell It On the Mountain
22. We Wish You a Merry Christmas

## CRAZY CAROLS

Give members of your youth group some crazy musical instruments like a kazoo, sand blocks, a "slide-a-phone" (a toy whistle that you can play tunes on), and so on. Then have the musicians play their rendition of a carol like "I'm Dreaming of a White Christmas." The results are hilarious.

## GIFT GRABBER

Here is a different way to "open gifts" at this year's Christmas Party. It works best with fifteen to twenty people. Everyone must bring a wrapped gift to begin with. They should be joke gifts and absolutely worthless, like an old shoe, an old motel key, etc. After the gifts are distributed, deal out an entire deck of playing cards, so that everyone has an equal number of cards. The leader should have a second deck of cards that he keeps. When everyone has a gift and some cards, the leader should shuffle his deck, draw one card, and announce what it is. Whoever has that card (from the first deck) should give the leader that identical card and then may help himself to any other person's gift. Then the next card should be announced by the leader, and the possessor of that identical card may help himself to someone else's gift, and so on until the whole deck of cards is used up. At first one person might accumulate several, but as his cards are exhausted, the momentum shifts. Of course, whoever has the gifts at the end of the game gets to unwrap them and keep them. Sometimes seeing what actually was the content of some of the packages that were most furiously sought after produces as much fun as the game itself.

## HO HO HO GAME

This is a crazy game for Christmas which is good for a lot of laughs (literally). One person should lie down on the floor (on his or her back), and the next person should lie down with his or her head on the first person's stomach, and the next person should lie down with his or her head on that person's stomach, and so on.

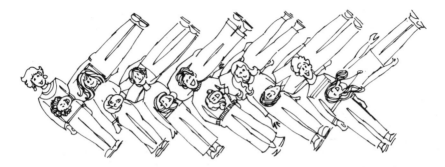

After everyone is down on the floor, the first person must say "Ho," the second person must say "Ho-Ho," and the third must say "Ho-Ho-Ho" and so on, with each person adding another "Ho" each time. It is to be done seriously, and if anyone goofs it by giggling or missing the correct number of "Ho's," the group must start over. It's really hilarious.

## HOLIDAY FUND RAISERS

Here are two good ideas for fund raising that are ideal for youth groups at Christmas. The first is to provide a gift-wrapping service for the church. The kids can charge a certain amount per gift and can also deliver the gift for an extra charge.

The second idea is to institute a "Christmas card sorting service." Church members can bring their cards for other church members to the church, and the youth group will sort them so that families can pick up all the cards for them on Sunday morning. The sender doesn't have to pay postage but instead pays a fee according to the number of cards that they send.

In both of the above ideas, the key to success is to make sure that they are promoted well and that the service provided is top notch. Most church members will appreciate the effort and will want to support the group by taking advantage of these services.

## HOLIDAY QUIZ

Here's a good game idea that will help everyone learn more about each other's Christmas. You will have to know in advance who will be in attendance, and you will have to contact everyone in order to make up the questions. But the result will be worth it. The questions below were used at a Christmas Party for a church choir. You could make up any questions that would be appropriate for your group. When the game is played, print up the questions, pass them out and set a time limit. Correct answers must be obtained by milling around and asking people for information. It's a lot of fun.

1. How will the eggs be served at Ann Cheatham's house Christmas a.m.? (A) All scrambled. (B) Over light. (C) 2 fried, 1 scrambled. (D) Fix their own!
2. On Christmas morning, Tom plans to have a cup of: (A) Tea. (B) Coffee. (C) Onion soup. (D) Sugar.
3. Will the Don Clarks have a *real* or *artificial* tree this year?
4. Leroy Chamberlin plans to have: (A) Two. (B) Four. (C) Five. (D) Six strings of lights on his family tree.
5. The presents at Betty Meyer's house will be opened: (A) Christmas Eve. (B) Christmas Day. (C) After Christmas dinner.
6. Pauline Haupt's favorite Christmas carol is: (A) "Joy to the World." (B) "O Come, All Ye Faithful." (C) "Silent Night."
7. Kathleen Brown's favorite Christmas cookie is a: (A) Christmas "tree." (B) Chocolate chip. (C) Mincemeat. (D) Sugar.
8. The big meal at the Crawford's house will be eaten on Christmas Eve and Carrol says that the leftovers will be eaten by: (A) Christmas Day. (B) Day after Christmas. (C) December 27. (D) The day that Tom comes over.
9. Will Harry Millard take a nap Christmas afternoon? (A) Absolutely. (B) Only if Twilla does. (C) Not with all the company they have.
10. We all know that Aaron Cheatham's favorite Christmas pie is: (A) Pumpkin. (B) Apple with a slice of cheese. (C) Cherry. (D) Mincemeat.
11. For Christmas dinner Dot Harrington will serve: (A) Turkey. (B) Ham. (C) Roast. (D) Steak.
12. When will Martha Aiken's tree come down? (A) The day after Christmas. (B) New Year's Eve. (C) January 2.
13. Polly Jacob's favorite Christmas decoration is a: (A) Nativity scene. (B) A snowman with sequined eyes. (C) A flashing star on top of the tree.
14. What will Martha Jackson use to wrap the most special present she will give? (A) Red Santa Claus wrap. (B) Red, green, and gold paper. (C) Silver bells in the design of the paper.
15. If money were no object, Dan Killinger would buy the woman in his life a: (A) Rolls Royce. (B) Lear Jet. (C) Hawaii. (D) ITT.
16. How will Bob Posno spend Christmas afternoon? (A) Nap time. (B) With seven and 3/4 grandchildren. (C) Football games on TV.

## HOLIDAY SIGNATURES

This is a mixer that can be used with any age group. It's easy and fun to play. Give each person a sheet of paper and a pencil. The left-hand border of the paper should have the letters in a word or phrase selected because of its association with the holiday or the occasion of the party. For example, at a Christmas Party, the words written down the side might be "Merry Christmas."

On a signal, the players should go around getting the signatures of the other players. They should try to find someone whose first or last name begins with one of the letters in the key word or phrase. When someone is found, she is asked to sign next to the appropriate letter. The first person to get signatures next to all of the letters on her sheet is the winner. If no winner has come forth after a certain period of time, stop the game, and whoever has found the most signatures will be the winner. In case of a tie, first names that match are worth more than last names—so the most matching first names wins. For larger groups, the phrase can be longer; for smaller groups, shorter.

## HUMAN CHRISTMAS TREE

Divide the group into teams and give each team plenty of Christmas tree decorations (lights, balls, tinsel, construction paper, etc.). Each team should select one of its members to be decorated like a tree. Set a time limit (10 minutes maximum), and whichever team does the best and most creative job of decorating their "human Christmas tree" will be the winner.

## INDOOR HAYRIDE

Here's a great idea for a way to have a hayride during lousy weather, or for a different way to go Christmas caroling. This way even groups in urban or suburban areas can still experience a hayride.

Secure a school bus without any seats, a panel truck, or a van and dump two feet of loose straw inside. Add an old fashioned pump organ, banjo, or accordian for effect and bring a supply of cider and fresh apples for eats. (CAUTION: Make sure there are windows for ventilation. The dust gets very dense without it!) When you are done, back up to a trash dumpster and sweep it all away.

## JINGLE BELLS

This is a great way to put new life into an old Christmas song. Divide into six groups and assign each group a phrase of the first verse of "Jingle Bells."

1. Dashing through the snow
2. In a one horse open sleigh
3. O'er the fields we go
4. Laughing all the way
5. Bells on bobsled ring
6. Making spirits bright

Each group should be instructed to decide upon words, actions, or both to be done by their group when their phrase is sung. For example, the group that has "Laughing all the way" might hold their stomachs and say "Ho, Ho, Ho." The entire group should sing the chorus (Jingle Bells, Jingle Bells, etc.) together and then the first verse. As each phrase in the verse is sung, the assigned group stands, does its part, and sits down. Do it several times, getting a little faster each time through.

## MERRY MIXER

Give each person a card with one letter of "Merry Christmas" printed on it. Then have the group mix up and regroup with people who have the other letters needed to spell the phrase. The first group to have all the letters is the winner and must scream,

"Merry Christmas!" This game will work best with a large group, and it can be used for other holidays by using the appropriate holiday greeting. With a small group, each person may have two or three letters.

## MUSICAL GIFT UNWRAP

Have everyone sit in a circle. Wrap a gift ahead of time with a great deal of paper, tape, string, ribbon, and whatever you can put on it to make it as difficult as possible to unwrap. (The gift could be in a small box which is wrapped inside a series of larger boxes.) Then give the gift to someone in the circle and start the music (Christmas music, of course).

As the music plays, the gift should be handed around the circle from person to person until the music stops. Whoever has the gift when the music stops must try to unwrap it as fast as possible, until the music starts again, and then the gift must continue on around the circle. Each time the music stops, someone gets to try and unwrap it, so that the gift will be unwrapped a little at a time. Try to make the time that each person is unwrapping the gift short enough so that they don't get very far. As soon as someone succeeds in totally unwrapping the gift, that person should be awarded the gift as a prize.

## NAME THAT CHRISTMAS CAROL

Here's a fun game that is based on the TV version of "Name That Tune." Divide into two teams. Each team should select one of its members to be the first contestant. When they are ready, have a pianist (or any other instrumentalist) play the first note of a Christmas carol. The contestant from Team #1 should try to guess the song. If he or she misses, the first two notes of the carol should be played and the contestant from Team #2 must take a guess. If wrong, three notes should be played, and the contestant from Team #1 should try again, and so on, back and forth until one of them guesses correctly. The scoring can go something like this:

If guessed correctly after 1 note  = 15 points
                                     2 notes = 10 points
                                     3 notes =  8 points
                                     4 notes =  6 points
                                     5 notes =  4 points
                                     6 notes =  2 points

If no one guesses it after six notes, just go on to the next song. Alternate back and forth as to which team goes first. Teams must send up a different contestant for each new song.

A variation of this would be to have the teams go separately, giving each new song to only one team. If they guess it after one note, they get 15 points; after two notes, 10 points; and so on. Carols can be chosen by drawing at random from a hat. This is a good game for a youth group meeting or party.

## ONE-ARMED GIFT WRAP

This is a good crowd breaker. Have three couples come up to the front and give them some paper, tape, string, ribbon, a pair of scissors, and a box to wrap. Tell them they must wrap the package together but the boys may only use their left hands and the girls only their right hands. Each must keep his other hand behind his back. Set a time limit. The couple with the best-wrapped package will be the winner.

## PIN THE NOSE ON RUDOLPH

Out of brown paper cut a large reindeer. Color it to look like Rudolph the Red-Nosed Reindeer (but leave off his large red nose). Hang it up. Give each person in the group a large red nose with a pin through it. (Use tape if you don't have a "pinable" surface.) Have everyone line up. Blindfold the first person, spin him around a bit, and point him in the direction of the reindeer. He may use his hands to find the right place. The person to pin or tape the nose on Rudolph the closest to where it belongs wins.

## SANTA CLAUS LOOKALIKES

Select three guys to sit in chairs and position three girls in front of the guys. Blindfold the girls and give each of them a can of shaving cream. The object is for each girl to use the shaving cream to create a beard that resembles Santa Claus. The couple with the best looking Santa wins.

## SANTA RELAY

Divide the group into two teams and have them line up. At a distance away from the groups, place two bags (one for each team) with the following contents: a beard, a hat, shirt and pants (red, if possible), a pillowcase, a few toys, and a pair of boots. On "go," the first person must run to the bag, put on the beard and the clothes, stuff the toys in the pillow case, throw it over his shoulder, and say in a deep Santa voice, "Ho, ho, ho, Merry Christmas." He must then take the toys out of the pillow case, undress, put everything back in the bag, and run back to tag the second person. The first team finished wins.

## SANTA STUFF

This game takes a little advance preparation. Get two pairs of long underwear and dye them red. Make sure the long johns are large. Then at a Christmas party, divide the group into two teams. Give each team lots of small party balloons (the round ones work best). You will probably need about 100 balloons for each team. Also give each team one pair of long johns.

When the game begins, each team should have one of its members put on the long johns. The rest of the team should start blowing up the balloons. As the balloons are blown up, several members of the team must try to stuff as many balloons as possible into the long johns (worn by their team member). Balloons should be stuffed into the arms, legs, and everywhere. Give the teams about two minutes for this. Then after the balloons have been stuffed inside, add a beard and hat and take pictures of your two fat and jolly Santas. The next step would be to count the balloons inside the long johns. This can be done by taking a pin and by popping them one at a time while the group counts. Be careful that you only prick balloons and not something else. The team that had the most balloons inside the long johns would be the winner. Be prepared for lots of laughs.

## STATIC SNOW

For a fun activity that will give your group a "White Christmas," have your youth group get together in a small room. In advance, buy several large bags of white styrofoam beads and funnel them into a vacuum cleaner. Then hook the hose on so the vacuum cleaner blows. (Be sure to run a test blow before adding the styrofoam beads or you will blow dust over everyone.) Turn on the machine and spray the beads all over the room. The feather-weight beads will become charged with static electricity and stick to everything and everyone. They are difficult to clean up, but the effect is worth it. For a little more excitement, you might turn off all the lights so that the kids have no idea what is being sprayed on them.

## STOCKING STUFFERS

This is a relay in which each team receives a Christmas stocking and an identical assortment of items that will fit into the stocking. The items should be placed in a box about twenty feet away from the team. On a signal, the first person should run with the stocking to the box and try to get everything completely into the stocking. After she has succeeded, she must dump it all out into the box and return the stocking to the next person in line, who should do the same thing. The first team to have all its members stuff the stocking wins. Try to get enough items so that it will require a little careful "packing" to get it all in. It's a lot of fun.

## TAFFY PULL

A traditional Christmas activity that can be very popular with young people is a good old-fashioned Taffy Pull. It will take and keep kids occupied up to three hours and is a lot of fun. The recipe is as follows:

    2 lbs. white sugar (4 cups)
    1 pt. white molasses (Kern Light Corn Syrup)
    1 pt. sweet cream (light condensed cream or Carnation milk)
    Para Wax, size of a walnut

Mix the above mixture in a large pan. It can be doubled or tripled and you can use as many pans as you need for your size group. Let the mixture come to a boil, then add one tablespoon Knox Gelatin which has been dissolved in one cup of warm to hot water. Boiling will take from twenty to thirty minutes. Stir continuously. When it begins to boil, turn back heat about 1/3 to 1/2. Stir until a few drops harden into round balls when dropped into a buttered pan or cold water. The mixture should be a dark yellow and bubbly. Grease a pie tin and pour the mixture into it. Let it cool fifteen to thirty minutes outside in cold weather or in a refrigerator. When it gets hard enough to pull, grease hands (take all jewelry off fingers), cut in half the mixture in the pie tin, and have four people begin to tug (two people per half). It will take at least fifteen to twenty minutes of pulling before it can be cut and wrapped. Pull the taffy as if you and your partner are swimming with alternate strokes hand over hand. Cut the taffy as it changes to a lighter color, small sections at a time. Lay these sections on the table and have another individual cut them into ½ inch strips. While those out in the kitchen stir the pots, have the remainder of the group take wax paper and cut it into ¾ inch squares for the taffy to be wrapped in. Make sure you have enough. You can add flavors such as vanilla, orange, or peanut butter by adding the flavoring to the mixture after you have pulled for about ten to fifteen minutes. It's great fun if you last.

## THIS CHRISTMAS, I'M GETTING . . .

Here's a fun game for Christmas parties that involves trying to guess the "secret" to the game. Begin by cluing in at least one other person in the room so that you can get the game started. You will also need a Christmas package or some other item that you can toss around. You begin by saying, "This Christmas, I'm getting . . . (and you complete the sentence)." After doing this, you should toss the package to someone else (the person you clued in) and he will complete the sentence correctly. You should announce that he is correct, and that not everyone will know what she is getting for Christmas. You can tell the group that if they know the secret to the game they will know what they are getting. However, if they say the wrong thing, then they must stand up, and remain standing, until they "figure out" what they are getting for Christmas.

The package should be tossed to someone else in the room, and that person must try to complete the sentence. If she doesn't know the secret, then she will probably be wrong, and you must tell her to stand up. She can then toss the package back to you, and you can complete the sentence again (only differently this time). If she is paying attention, she should catch on before too long.

What is the secret? You must always complete the sentence with something that begins with your first and last initials. For example, if your name is Tom Douglas, then you might say, "For Christmas, I'm getting ten dollars" (or tiny deer, or tremendous daffodils, etc.) Some people will catch on right away, others will never catch on. It's a lot of fun.

## THE TWELVE DAYS OF CHRISTMAS

Divide the entire group into twelve small teams. Each team should think of something that their "true love gave to me" that will fit into the song, "The Twelve Days of Christmas." Each group must be assigned one of the twelve days. The items that they come up with can be anything: "Six stinky sewers," "Twelve green burritos," etc. Encourage the groups to be as creative and as wild as they can be. After each team

127

has had time to think of their "item," have the group sing the song. At the appropriate time in the song, each team should sing their item, and the song should continue.

## WHITE ELEPHANT GIFT AUCTION

Each person should bring a "White Elephant" gift, nicely wrapped, to this auction. The gift can be of any value but should be something from around the house that is no longer needed. Special "gag" type gifts can be purchased if a person cares to, but people should be encouraged not to spend a lot of money. All the gifts should then be placed under a Christmas tree or displayed at the front of the room so that everyone can examine them. People can feel, shake, or examine the gifts prior to the auction. Each person should be given a package of assorted "money" which can be in the form of poker chips, Monopoly game money, etc. Everyone should get a little different amount. You as a leader can act as the auctioneer, and you must auction off each gift to the highest bidder. You should make a big deal out of each gift and make wild speculations as to what the gift might be. Everyone may bid on each gift. Whoever wins the bidding on a particular gift, gets the gift and must open it in front of everyone. He may either keep it or sell it to someone else for the price he paid for it or more. If he sells the gift to someone else, then he can bid again on another gift. Once a person has a gift, he cannot bid on another. He may, if he wants to, give his extra money to a friend who doesn't have a gift yet. That makes the value of the gifts keep rising.

## WRAP THE DUCK

This is a great Christmas Party idea, if you have access to some live ducks. Have couples compete to see which team can "gift wrap" a duck the best in a two-minute (or so) time limit. Provide wrapping paper, ribbon, tape, etc., but no boxes. Make sure that the kids do not hurt the ducks (squashing them or whatever), and this can be really fun to watch. Other animals work just as well, such as chickens or rabbits. Have the rest of the group decide who is the winning couple.

## SCRAMBLED CHRISTMAS

Give everyone in the group a piece of paper and a pencil. Instruct the group to write Merry Christmas at the top of their papers. Then give them four minutes to write down as many words as possible using the letters in that holiday phrase. The person with the most words wins.

## YOUTH GROUP CHRISTMAS SHOPPING DAY

Set aside a day before Christmas (as early as possible, but when the kids in the youth group are out of school) to take the whole youth group Christmas shopping together. Many times kids cannot buy Christmas gifts for the family without little brother or sister watching, or they don't really know where to go or what to buy. This can be a fun activity for the group, plus the kids can help each other shop. They should bring their money, and together you can go to a large shopping area. Afterwards, the kids can help each other wrap their gifts and have some refreshments. This works best with junior highers.

# Creative Communication

## A LITTLE GIRL LOOKS AT THE CHRISTMAS STORY

Here's a short one-act play for Christmas that can be done with only two people. There is a lady (Mrs. Hansen), and a little girl (Laney Joy). The father is just a man's voice off-stage. The girl can be anyone dressed like a little girl and acting like one. For best results the lines should be memorized. The set doesn't have to be too elaborate—just a make-shift living room with a front door and perhaps a couch and some other simple furnishings.

Laney:     (Singing) "Away in a manger, no crib for a bed,
                       The little Lord Jesus laid down his sweet head.
                       The stars in the sky looked down where he lay,
                       The little Lord Jesus, asleep on the hay.
                       The cattle are lowing, the baby awakes,
                       But little Lord Jesus, no crying he makes . . ."
           (Doorbell rings.)

Father:    Laney . . . Laney Joy! Will you get the door?

Laney:     I would, dad . . . but what if it's not a friendly person?

Father:    It's probably Mrs. Hansen. Just tell her to wait downstairs until I'm finished with this appointment.

Laney:     (Opens door.) Hello, lady.

Lady:      (Very cheerfully) Well, hello. You must be the preacher's little girl . . . I'm Mrs. Hansen . . . from church. I have an appointment with your dad. May I come in?

Laney:     He's already got one 'pointment upstairs. I don't think he needs another one.

| | |
|---|---|
| *Lady:* | I don't think you understand, dear . . . You see— |
| *Laney:* | In fact, I am certain that he does not need any. My mama always says that papa has too many 'pointments. |
| *Lady:* | *(Mildly amused)* No, dear, you don't understand. I want to talk to your daddy . . . about marrying my daughter. |
| *Laney:* | Oh, lady, you're too late. My papa is already married. He married my mama a couple of years ago. |
| *Lady:* | A *couple* of years? |
| *Laney:* | Yes, lady. I think it was even before I was born . . . and I'm five years old. |
| *Lady:* | Yes . . . I'm sure it was— |
| *Father:* | Laney. Is that Mrs. Hansen? |
| *Laney:* | Yes, sir. I'm trying to tell her that you aren't innerested in marrying . . . |
| *Father:* | Laney, just invite her in. I'll be with her in a few minutes. |
| *Laney:* | Well . . . it's against my better judgment. But I guess I have to do what my papa says. Come in. While we are waiting I will entertain you. |
| *Lady:* | Oh, that's not necessary, dear. |
| *Laney:* | Oh, yes, lady. It's part of my role as the preacher's daughter. First I will tell you about myself. My name is Laney Joy, and I'm five years old . . . and I'm a very precarious child. |
| *Lady:* | *(Whispered)* I'm beginning to see that. *(Aloud)* Precarious? |
| *Laney:* | Yes. That means I'm ahead of other kids my same age. I can sing . . . and I can read the Bible all by myself. |
| *Lady:* | Read the Bible? And you're only five? |
| *Laney:* | Aren't you impressed, lady? Would you like to hear me read something? |
| *Lady:* | Well, I . . . uh . . . |
| *Laney:* | I know. Since it is nearly Christmas, I will read the Christmas story to you. Have you heard that one? |
| *Lady:* | Yes, a few times. |
| *Laney:* | But I bet you've never heard it the way I read it. |
| *Lady:* | Somehow I can believe that! |
| *Laney:* | O.K. This is how it goes.<br>Once upon a time, a long time ago, an angel came to Mary and said, "Mary, would you like to have the baby Jesus?" Mary said she guessed she would someday, after she married Joseph. But she did not know if she would name her first son Jesus. But the angel said that was not what he had in mind. He wanted to know if she would have the Son of God. Well, Mary did not know about that. She said she would have to think about it. |
| *Lady:* | Wait. Are you sure that's the way the story goes? |

Laney:   Certainly. You don't think she would agree to something like that without thinking about it first, do you?

Lady:    I guess I never thought of it quite that way.

Laney:   You have to think about these things, lady . . . Anyway, Mary finally said she guessed it would be O.K., as long as she could wait until she married Joseph. Then they would want to wait until they had enough money to support a baby. But the angel said, "No way. Don't you ever read your Bible, Mary? 'Cause in the Bible it says that Jesus was born at just the right time. And that right time is right now." So Mary had to make up her mind quick. It was one of those now-or-never deals. You know about them, don't you, lady?

Lady:    Well, yes. But not quite in that way . . . So Mary decided to have the baby Jesus?

Laney:   I was just coming to that next part. Mary said it would be O.K. with her if it was O.K. with Joseph. You can kinda see how he might not like it, can't you, lady?

Lady:    I never thought about it before, but, yes, I can.

Laney:   Well, the angel said if she was really worried about it, he would appear to Joseph in a dream and tell him all about it. But would she please make up her mind because he had to go on and do other things for God. So then Mary said O.K., she'd do it if the angel would promise her that everything would be all right. But you know what the angel said to that?

Lady:    No, I don't.

Laney:   The angel said he did not know what would happen. He only knew what God said to do. But he reckoned if Mary did what God wanted her to do, chances were things would turn out O.K. in the end. Then he quoted Hebrews 11:1 to her and left . . . So that's how it all began. Then you know what happened?

Lady:    I used to think I did, but I'm not so sure now.

Laney:   Well, next, Mary and Joseph had to go to Bethlehem to pay up their back taxes. You see, God had to get them to Bethlehem so what Micah had said would come true—about Jesus being born in Bethlehem—and God figured taxes were as good an excuse as any . . . My papa's been to the Holy Land—that's where Bethlehem is—and he says that's a hard trip even in a jeep. So you can imagine what it was like on a donkey. I bet by the time they got to Bethlehem Mary was sorry she ever got involved in the whole business. But that's not the kind of thing you can change your mind about; so she had to go through with it. But by the time they got to Bethlehem, I bet she was not singing that same song.

Lady:    Song? What song is that?

Laney:   'Bout how her soul doth magnify the Lord. She was probably saying she'd just as soon somebody else had all that honor and let her just be a plain housewife—which was all she ever wanted anyway. You know, in one way it would have been nice if God could have waited 'til today and let some woman's lib lady have baby Jesus. But that was not God's style. He wanted Mary to do it. So they got to Bethlehem, but all the hotels were full 'cause Joseph hadn't phoned ahead for reservations. Then you know what happened?

Lady: They had to stay in a stable?

Laney: That's very good, lady. They had to stay in a stable 'cause there was not room for them in the Holiday Inn. Well, the angel was looking down at them, and you know what he did? . . . He told God he did not think it was fair, making them have it so rough. And he offered to go down with a whole squad of other angels and sort of clean up the place, and make it a little better looking since it would be the first place baby Jesus would see on earth. And if it was too bad, it might make Him change His mind and decide not to live on earth, after all. Well, God said that would be a shame, 'cause the world was counting on Jesus. But He would not let the angels come and fix things up. He said He'd already taken care of that.

Lady: Oh? How had He done that?

Laney: He made baby Jesus be just like any other human baby, so He wouldn't notice if He was born in a stable or a house or a palace. The angels said they guessed that was all right—they had not thought of it that way. Which is why God is God— 'cause He had a better idea . . . Then the exciting part happened.

Lady: And what was that?

Laney: That was when the angels started singing "Glory to God in the Highest." The shepherds heard it, and they started singing "Do You Hear What I Hear?" Then the—

Lady: Now, wait a minute. I think you're confusing your stories.

Laney: I just elaborated a little, that's all. It *could* have happened. Anyway, the little drummer boy heard it, and he started playing his drum. And that was the first Christmas concert. All these people went to the stable and . . . Oh, lady, it was so exciting! *(Excitement builds, growing into awe.)* They saw baby Jesus . . . and they knew He was the Son of God . . . and they—Lady, can you imagine what it was like? The Son of God on earth! So God would know what it was like to be a man . . . 'cause that was the only way He could ever save people from their sins. Oh, lady, it must have been wonderful!

Lady: *(Getting caught up in it, too)* Yes, it must have been!

Laney: I guess it was 'bout as wonderful as it is today.

Lady: Huh? As *what* is today?

Laney: As finding out that God came to earth.

Lady: *(Slightly puzzled)* Finding out that God came. . . ? *(She understands.)* Oh. Yes. I guess it *was* almost as exciting as that. And that's mighty exciting!

Laney: Yes, lady. That's the truth! I cannot think of anything—

Father: Good-bye, Mr. Petersen. Hope I was able to help . . . *(Louder)* Mrs. Hansen, I can see you now.

Lady: Yes, pastor, I'll be right in . . . Laney Joy, thanks for the story.

Laney: Oh, that's all right, lady. Any time. *(Laney resumes her song.)* "Away in a manger, no crib for a bed . . ." *(Fade)*

## CHRIST TREE

This Christmas try this simple suggestion for decorating your Christmas tree. After a short discussion about the symbols Christ used for Himself and the symbols others have used, have each young person make several tree ornaments representing Jesus Christ. Be sure to have available plenty of construction paper, marking pens, scissors, tape, etc. You will be amazed at how many different ornaments your kids can come up with.

## CHRISTMAS CARDS FOR JESUS

Here's a good idea for a Christmas youth group meeting that will really get the kids involved. Have them create a "Christmas Card for Jesus" using construction paper, scenes from magazines and old cards, plus sayings or verses that they make up. Have the kids think in terms of what they would say on a card if it were going to be sent to Jesus on His birthday. Stress creativity and originality and allow the group plenty of time to complete the cards. You might also ask the kids to present a "gift" to Jesus along with the card. After they have finished, the kids can read the cards and show them to each other or simply put them on display. The results will be very exciting.

## CHRISTMAS CARD ORNAMENTS

At Christmas time, put a Christmas tree (either real or artificial) in the church foyer. Place a few decorations on the tree but leave it embarrassingly bare. Leave a package of ornament hangers under the tree, along with a donation box, decorated to look like a gift. Ask the people of the church to consider hanging one of their Christmas cards on the tree, with greetings to the entire congregation, as an alternative to sending out individual cards to everyone. The card can be hung on the tree by using one of the ornament hangers provided. Also ask them to donate the money that would be saved by not buying so many cards and by not paying so much postage to whatever worthy project you happen to have. The money can be deposited in the gift box under the tree. Of course, people can give more than the money they save if they choose.

People are generally more responsive to this if you have a specific project in mind, such as a missionary project, providing toys or other gifts for an orphanage, giving to a hunger relief agency, etc. Be sure to stress that this project is optional. If people would rather send personal greeting cards, they should be encouraged to do so.

## CHRISTMAS FIELD TRIP

Take your young people to a shopping center and turn them loose at one of the peak periods during the Christmas shopping season. Their assignment should be to scatter among the shoppers and observe what is happening as people select gifts. As often as possible encourage the kids to talk to shoppers and to ask them what they are hoping to give and receive as gifts. Also, the kids should observe what the stores are really pushing, what items they feel are inappropriate for Christmas gifts, and what effect music or lack of it in the stores has on the mood of the shoppers. After thirty minutes of observing, return to a prearranged place and share what you learned.

## CHRISTMAS LOCK-IN

If you are looking for a significant and meaningful activity for your youth group (ninth grade and above), the Christmas Lock-in is it. The Christmas Lock-in is a thirty-six-hour event that is held one week before Christmas on a Friday and Saturday. Here is the schedule:

*Friday*

*7:00 p.m.:* Contemporary Worship Service - run entirely by the kids and focusing on the practical meaning of Christmas.

*8:00 p.m.:* Free time for socializing.

*9:00 p.m.:* Doors are locked and the work begins. Begin by making favors for the nursing home that the kids will be visiting Saturday. Then wrap gifts for poor families and the children at Children's Hospital (or the children's ward of any hospital.) After that, pack food baskets for the poor (get the food from a congregational door collection along with funds raised by the youth themselves). The food that is purchased for the food baskets should be bought during a midnight shopping spree.

*After midnight:* The kids sleep in the church.

*Saturday*

*8:00 a.m.:* Breakfast.

*9:00 a.m.:* Deliver baskets to the poor.

*11:30 a.m.:* Lunch.

*1:00 p.m.:* Carol singing and favors given out at nursing home.

*3:00 p.m.:* Carol singing and gifts distributed at Children's Hospital.

*6:00 p.m.:* Dinner.

*7:00 p.m.:* Caroling to church members' homes.

*9:00 p.m.:* Gala Christmas party with lots of singing, fellowship, and close with Communion.

## CHRISTMAS TREE GIFTS

This strategy is designed to help young people examine the values expressed in giving and receiving gifts and is obviously most appropriate during the Christmas season. Print up copies of the Christmas tree drawing (shown below) on letter size paper so that everyone will have one. Second best would be to have the kids draw a reasonable facsimile.

Each person should then "trim" his or her tree with symbolic drawings or words according to the instructions below:

1. On the "banner" around the tree, write a Christmas message that you would like to give to the world.
2. In space two, draw the best gift you ever got at Christmas—something so special that it is a high point in your Christmas memories.

3. Next, draw the gift that you would like to receive this Christmas more than anything else. You don't have to be realistic here—it can be anything.
4. Draw a gift that you gave to someone else that was especially appropriate and appreciated.
5. Draw the gift that you would bring to the manger. (Remember the wise men?) Let your gift say something about how you see Christ and your relationship to Him.
6. Symbolize some of the gifts that God has given to you in the sixth space.
7. At the base of the tree, write out some of the feelings that this exercise may have stirred up. What is the purpose of giving? Why do we give at Christmas? Do you feel uncomfortable about some of the drawings you have made? Do you feel pride? Thanksgiving?

After the exercise, a discussion or voluntary sharing time may be appropriate. You may want to divide into small groups and allow each person to share what he or she drew or wrote on their Christmas tree.

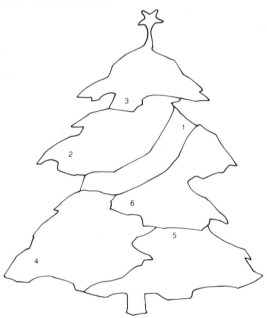

## CHRISTMAS MISSIONARY DINNER

For this special Christmas activity, have your youth group select some missionaries abroad that the church supports. The group should get to know the missionaries they have chosen by corresponding with them and by reading their newsletters. Then begin making plans for a _____ ry Dinner" sometime in November or early December. There sho_____ ___as decorations and pictures or letters from the missionaries posted s_____ le can see them. The youth group can cook and serve the meal, which could ___ lude some dishes from the country where the missionaries are serving. Adults of the church should be invited to the dinner. Following a talent show by the youth and a presentation of the work being done by the missionaries, the people may be asked to give a free-will offering. The offering can then be sent to the missionaries as a "Christmas Bonus," which they ordinarily would not get. It is a good idea to hold this event as early as possible (even early November) as it could take a long time before the money reaches the missionaries.

## CHRISTMAS MITTEN TREE

A good Christmas project for a youth group would be to sponsor a "Christmas Mitten Tree." Families of the church should be encouraged to bring in a pair of mittens which they have bought or made to decorate a tree which will be provided by the youth group. The mittens can then be given to a local orphanage.

## CHRISTMAS TELEGRAMS

Have each person print the letters *MERRY CHRISTMAS* vertically down the left hand margin of a sheet of paper. Then tell everyone to compose a Christmas telegram, with the words of the telegram beginning with each of the letters down the left margin of their sheet. In other words, the first word would begin with "M," the second with "E," and so on. After all have finished, have the group share their creations. They can be either serious or funny.

## CHRISTMAS TREE OF LOVE

Here's a good way to encourage members of your youth group or congregation to cut down on the amount of money that they spend on gifts for each other and to use that money to give to missions, relief, and other needs at home and abroad. To help people identify those needs, put up a "Christmas Tree of Love," which could be a flat cardboard tree (painted green) or a real tree. On the tree hang ornaments that can be removed. Each ornament should have a written project on it that needs a specific amount of money or other type of help. The people should be asked to take an ornament from the tree and make that their Christmas project. If you use a real tree, you could ask the people to replace each ornament they take with another, as a sign that another need has been met. Make sure that the ornaments represent a wide variety of giving opportunities for people, in both large and small amounts.

## CHRISTMAS TREE TRACTS

Secure permission to decorate a tree in a shopping mall or other public place. At least six weeks before Christmas, write to the American Bible Society to find out what Scripture leaflets (sold below cost for just a few cents) are available for the Christmas season. They usually have a good selection. Their address is:

American Bible Society
Volunteer Activities, Dept. YS
1865 Broadway
New York, NY 10023

If you live in a Spanish-speaking area, buy some Spanish selections also. Wrap the leaflets "tootsie roll" fashion in colored cellophane and dangle them from the tree. Arrange for your youth choir or other musicians (or a good tape recorder when live music is not available) to furnish background music. Also line up a person to "man the tree," to invite people to "Take One!" and to answer questions. You'll need a supply of extra ornaments to replenish the tree.

Christmas is a special time to communicate God's love. This can be one effective way to do it.

## CHRISTMAS VACATION

Below is a list of things that a person might do during Christmas vacation. Have the kids think of some other possibilities and add them to the list. Then have the kids (individually) categorize the items in the following manner:

X - This is definitely *NOT* for me
U - Unlikely that I would do it
N - Neutral or unsure
P - Possibly I would do this in the future
A - I affirm this; I will definitely try to build it into my life, if I have not already done so

_____ 1. Worked up a show and performed it in a hospital ward.

_____ 2. Made up a basket of food and delivered it to a needy family.

_____ 3. Organized a group to go caroling in the neighborhood.

_____ 4. Invited some children from an underprivileged area to spend a day with me and returned the visit.

_____ 5. Wrote many letters to go out with Christmas cards to friends in many different parts of the country and world.

_____ 6. Organized a block party for New Year's Eve where everyone brought some food dish to share with each other.

_____ 7. Enjoyed it just with my family.

_____ 8. Made the decorations for our tree.

_____ 9. Repaired some broken toys to be distributed to children in an orphanage.

_____ 10. Solicited friends, relatives, and neighbors for old clothes to send to needy families.

_____ 11. Contributed substantially to a dozen different organizations which appealed for funds.

_____ 12. Devoted a whole day to helping some other student complete a term paper; but not doing it for him.

_____ 13. At the year's end, evaluated how the year had gone and made plans to make the next year more significant.

_____ 14. Made with my own hands almost all the presents I gave.

_____ 15. Sat down and wrote some letters to public figures affirming a position they had recently taken, or acknowledged a beautiful act of some other person.

_____ 16. Bought a ticket to a play for a child who had never seen one.

_____ 17. Attempted, without moralizing, to pose alternatives on some basic issues of our time, like the nuclear arms race, economics, ecology, energy, etc. to friends and relatives.

_____ 18. Tried to lift the usual level of family relationships to a higher plane in keeping with the season.

_____ 19. Avoided taking the path of least resistance in present giving, and really tried to find out what the various receivers would enjoy.

_____ 20. Went out of my way to help children in the neighborhood capture a less materialistic and more spiritual significance to the holiday season.

After the kids have done this, you can follow up with a discussion. You might also pick several items and see if you can do them together as a group. It's a good way for kids to set a few priorities for themselves at Christmas.

## DO-IT-YOURSELF CHRISTMAS CARDS

Why not have your group make their own Christmas cards this year? Use a simple block-printing technique, a collage on construction paper, or if your group is really talented, get into silk screening. Here are some ways to use the cards.

1. If you can make enough, package them in bundles of five or ten and sell them to members of your congregation as a fund raiser to buy presents for needy children.
2. Ask your pastor for a list of the shut-ins in your congregation and assign each young person one or two names to send a card to.
3. Send cards to every patient in a nearby nursing home or the pediatric ward of your local hospital.

## DRIVE-THROUGH NATIVITY

Here is an idea that really makes the Christmas story live. Set up a number of nativity scenes using kids from your group as well as live animals. Make the scenes as authentic as possible. Each scene should have its own 4 x 8 sign, designed as a scroll with appropriate Scripture verses. Also, the use of colored lights can be very effective.

People should view the scenes from their cars. When they drive through they should be met at the welcome point with a program explaining the scenes. Cars should proceed through the scenes with lights out. The route can be outlined with luminarios. A "luminario" is a paper bag containing two to three inches of sand in the bottom. Inside is a six-inch candle placed in the center. (Make sure the side of the bag is taller than the candle.) After viewing all the scenes, the cars will pass the exit point where they should be thanked for coming and reminded to turn on their lights. In addition to the nativity scenes, it is a good idea to show a film about Christmas in a building about once every twenty minutes. The people can come view the film, then drive through the scenes. The drive-through should run continuously for two hours. Kids can work one-hour shifts.

It is really important to publicize the event to the entire community via newspapers, TV, radio, etc. Families really appreciate the scenes, especially if you do them two or three days before Christmas to coincide with people who are out doing last minute shopping or looking at Christmas lights and decorations. Any Christmas scenes will work: (1) Mary and Joseph on their way to Bethlehem, (2) the traditional manger scene, (3) The wise men following the star, and (4) the appearance of the angels to the shepherds. This event is very effective and can become not just a church event, but a community tradition.

## EXMAS IN ACREMA

Here's a great idea for Christmas that can either be read as a sermon, duplicated and discussed after everyone has read it, or even narrated while being acted out. Here are some questions for discussion that might be used after the story is read:

1. If you could control Christmas, what would you change?
2. What would you consider a good way to keep Exmas and Crissmas from getting confused?
3. Do you think it would be best for the church just to cancel Christmas and celebrate Christ's birth some other time?
4. What is the best way to get people to understand the real meaning of Christmas? Advertising, church pageants, or what?

A Letter Home:

My travels have taken me to a strange and wonderful country called Acrema. It is a land of many contradictions. It has high mountains, yet flat plains. It has vast open spaces, yet cities crammed with people. It even has a holiday filled with contradictions—a holiday called Exmas.

Preparations for this festival last for over fifty days and yet on the one day of what is supposed to be celebration, there is more quiet than merriment. It is difficult to determine whether the holiday itself or the preparation for it is the reason for the season. The preparations are very strange. They begin when people purchase tremendous quantities of cardboard cards with pictures and messages on them. The pictures are of various subjects. Some portray snow scenes; some depict fireplaces; some have quite a modern tone; some are pictures of the way Acremans believe their ancestors lived. The pictures convey no central theme. The messages inside the cards are equally nebulous. Most often they say, "Seasons Greetings," which could be said at any time of the year. It is very difficult to say what the whole Exmas Season is supposed to represent. Some have proposed that its name be changed to "Great Religious Leader's Day" and that it be celebrated the fourth Monday of December. Although the cards are seemingly innocuous and vague, they cause untold suffering. The Acreman keeps long lists, which are called Exmas Card Lists. A card is sent to everyone on the list. Great care is taken that no one on the list is missed. Apparently some curse is associated with neglecting someone. When the task is finally finished and the cards are mailed, the Acreman sighs with relief and gives thanks to the gods that the task is over for one more year. All is peaceful then, as the Acreman receives cards which his friends have mailed him, unless he receives one from someone to whom he did not send an Exmas Card. Then there is much wailing and cursing of the gods as the Acreman pulls on his overcoat and boots, drives through unspeakably crowded streets to the equally crowded marketplace and mails the Exmas card that was forgotten.

An equally strange custom is the purchase of Exmas Gifts. This is a very difficult procedure. Another list is made, after which an elaborate guessing game begins. Every citizen has to guess the value of the gift which every friend will send him so that he may send one of equal value, whether he can afford it or not. And they buy as gifts for one another such things as no man ever bought for himself. The sellers, understanding the custom, put forth all kinds of trumpery, and whatever, being useless and ridiculous, they have been unable to sell throughout the year, they now sell as an Exmas Gift. And although the Acremans profess to lack sufficient necessary things, such as metal, leather, wood, and paper, an incredible quantity of these things is being wasted every year, being made into gifts. When the gifts are exchanged, gratitude must be profusely expressed. Though the gifts are often useless and the gratitude is largely insincere, the Acreman must manufacture a show of delight. He even has to grind out written notes to express his unfelt "gratitude." The sellers of the gifts, as well as the buyers, become exceedingly exhausted from the strain of the crowds and traffic. They are frantic in their attempts to finish everything on time and yet are in constant need of stopping and resting. This frenzied state, in their barbaric language, is known as the Exmas Rush. The people become pale and weary so that any stranger visiting Acrema at this time of the year would suppose that some great calamity had befallen the land. When the day of the festival arrives, the Acremans, except those with young children, sleep until noon, being worn out from the Exmas Rush and the excesses of the Exmas Parties. In the evening of Exmas Day, they eat five times what they usually eat. The next day heads and stomachs are greatly distressed from the eating and the spirits consumed in excess.

The motivation for this strange behavior is most confusing to our best scholars. The motivation could not possibly be merriment, for most Acremans seem more weary than joyful.

Our best explanation is that their motivation must have its source in their pagan worship. Two deities seem particularly popular at this time. One is a weak, comical deity, represented by a man in a red suit and a long white beard. He seems to be a harmless totem of a worship of materialism. Only small children take him seriously. Adults usually greet this totem with a condescending smile.

The other object of worship centers around a very interesting contest of deities called bowls. Constant reference is made, wherever Acremans gather, to Super Bowls, Orange Bowls, Rose Bowls, Sugar Bowls, etc. It is probably named after the bowl-shaped headgear worn by the participants. Each deity is represented by some fierce animal, i.e., Bears, Lions, Rams, Falcons, etc. At the exact time coinciding with the Exmas Rush, these deities have annual contests to determine supremacy. At least weekly, the spiritual leaders of the households gather in large numbers at the actual site of the contest. Those unable to make the pilgrimage to the contest worship in front of family altars or receiving sets in their homes, urging their favorite deity on to victory. Hecataeus, a second-rate scholar, believes that these are not worship services, but only games that the people are playing. But no real scholar agrees with him. These contests are taken much too seriously to be mere games. Their statistics are chronicled much too thoroughly and remembered much too completely.

My opinion, which I share with many scholars, is that perhaps there is a connection between the worship of these deities and the annual ritual called the Exmas Rush. Perhaps the Exmas Rush is a type of self-flagellation the Acremans believe their deities require of them. Why else would the people punish themselves so? If it is not to help their deities, the Exmas Rush just doesn't make sense.

There is another group in Acrema, almost too small to be mentioned at all, that celebrate a completely different festival at this time of the year. They call their celebration Crissmas.

The celebration centers around an ancient story about a baby that was born of very special birth many, many years ago. The story has it that there were signs in the heavens proclaiming this baby's birth. This unusual baby grew into an extraordinary man. The story has it that this man could walk on water. He could heal the sick. He could open the eyes of the blind and raise the dead. His life was absolutely perfect. Many said he was the son of some God which they claimed was the only God. His life was cut short by execution. He was pronounced dead and buried. Those who believe in this person say that he came back from the dead and that he was reborn and went into the heavens. The believers in this occurance say that this person will come back again to judge the world. His followers claim that only those who believe in this will be forgiven.

So every Crissmas they remember again the birth of this one who is their "savior." They continue to retell the story of his birth. They use figures of his mother, of a baby born in a stable, and other helps in remembering his birth. They gather together on the eve of his birth date to sing and praise him. They light candles and say that he is the truth that came into the world as a small light and now illuminates the whole world in his truth. These people call themselves Crisstians, I assume after this beautiful holiday.

I talked to the priest of one of these groups and asked him why they celebrate Crissmas on the same day as Exmas. It seemed terribly confusing to me. He said that the date of Crissmas had long ago been established and that he had hoped that more Acremans would celebrate it as his group did, or that God would put it in their minds to celebrate Exmas on some other day or not at all. For Exmas and the Rush distracts the minds of even the few from sacred things. He was glad that men make merry at Crissmas, but in Exmas there is no merriment

141

left. And when I asked why Acremans endured the rush, he replied, "It is, O stranger, a racket," using the words (I suppose) of some ancient oracle and speaking unintelligibly to me (for the racket is an instrument which the barbarians use in a game called tennis).

Hecataeus, in his usual way of oversimplifying the facts, has formulated a hypothesis that Crissmas and Exmas are the same. This is utterly impossible. First of all, the pictures stamped on the Exmas Cards have nothing to do with the sacred story which the priests tell. Secondly, although most Acremans don't believe the religion of the few, they still send gifts and cards and participate in the Rush. It is unlikely that anyone would suffer so greatly for a God they did not know. Hecataeus's hypothesis also fails to account for the central event of the Exmas Season—the Bowls—the contests of the deities for supremacy. Something as important as the Bowls would not be allowed to continue if the people were trying to remember their God. No, my theory ties it all together, except those who celebrate Crissmas. They are the strange ones. I have no idea where their story could have originated —unless it actually did happen.

## HAND-MADE GIFTS

This is a good idea for camps or weekend retreats especially at Christmas. At the beginning of camp, have each person draw a name from a box containing everyone's name written on a slip of paper. Then ask each person to create a "gift" for the person whose name she drew. The gift should be completed by the end of camp or by some other specified time. Materials can be provided such as glue, paints, pieces of wood, metal, string, etc. The gifts can be made of anything but should be made with that special person in mind. No one should reveal who they are making their gift for until the time when the gifts are exchanged. At that time follow up with a discussion on giving and receiving or on the meaning of the various gifts that were created.

## HIGH-RISE HAYRIDE

Hayrides are possible even if you live in the city! Use trucks and fill them with hay and kids. A flat-bed "semi" truck and trailer can hold fifty to one hundred kids. Plan a route on not-so-busy streets and keep the speed down to 20 m.p.h. or less for safety. At Christmas you can go "caroling" at high-rise apartments or condominiums, and people will come out on their balconies to hear. It's a great way to spread a little "Christmas cheer."

## JOY TO THE AMAZING GRACE

If you get tired of singing the same old Christmas tunes this year, try leading the group in "Joy to the World" using the tune to "Amazing Grace." It works. Then sing "Amazing Grace" to the tune of "Joy to the World." There's a message there some-where!

## KEEPING CHRIST IN CHRISTMAS

This is an outline for a Christmas program that deals with the question, "Is it possible to see Christ in Christmas today?" It can be presented as a "man on the street" interview, with a reporter holding a microphone, with a TV camera, and with people walking back and forth as if shopping for Christmas gifts. The reporter can begin by saying something like: "Good evening, I'm Barry Harry, your man-on-the-street reporter, live from the corner of Fifth and Main St. where we're asking people, 'Just what does Christmas mean to you?' We want to find out if it is possible for anyone to still see Christ in the Christmas of today."

The reporter should stop various people as they walk by and ask them the above question. The responses can be as follows:

1. "Lights"
2. "Presents"
3. "Cards"
4. "Crowds"
5. "Music"
6. "Vacation"
7. "Parties"
8. "Family"
9. "Snow"
10. "Money"

Others may be added if you wish. Each person should talk a little bit about their answer. For example, the first person might say: "Lights. Christmas lights. They're everywhere! Lights on trees, lights on houses, lights on the streets. Red lights, green lights, blue lights, flashing lights, millions of lights. That's gotta be it. Lights."

After all these people have been interviewed, the reporter should turn to the camera and say, "Well, it's just as we thought. No one sees Christ in Christmas anymore. . . ." At that point, one more person can come up and ask what's going on, and the reporter should go ahead and ask that person the same question. "What does Christmas mean to you?" He or she should answer, "Christ, of course." The reporter should act surprised and say, "But how can you possibly see Christ in Christmas today?" The answer can go something like this:

"Well, when I see the *LIGHTS,* I see the One who came as the Light of the whole world. When I see the *PRESENTS,* I think of His presence in my life, and how He came as God's gift to the world. When I get a Christmas *CARD,* I think of how God "cared enough to send the very best." When I hear the *MUSIC,* I hear the angels singing on that first Christmas, and I think of how Christ brings harmony to a dissonant world. When I see all the *CROWDS,* I realize that every person is so important to God that He sent His Son to die for us. When I go to a *PARTY* or take a *VACATION,* I think of the celebration in heaven when anyone decides to follow Christ and how Jesus said, 'Come unto me all you who labor and are burdened down, and I will give you rest'—a vacation. When I'm with my *FAMILY,* I'm thankful to be adopted into the family of God through Christ, and when I see the *SNOW,* I know my sins have been washed whiter than snow. When I spend any of my *MONEY,* I think of the great price that was paid so that I can have treasures in heaven. In fact, just about everywhere I look, I see Christ."

The reporter then turns to the camera and says, "Well, it's just as we thought. It *IS* possible to see Christ in Christmas today . . . if you just open your eyes."

### LETTER FROM MARY AND JOSEPH

Here is a discussion starter that works well at Christmas. It can help kids to put themselves into the Christmas story and to understand it a little better. To begin, give the kids paper and pencils, and ask them to write a letter to a close friend. Tell the girls that they are to imagine that they are Mary, the mother of Jesus, just after she has found out that she is pregnant with Jesus. She should explain how she feels and how others feel toward her.

The boys should pretend that they are Joseph. Each one should write a letter to a close friend telling her how it feels to be engaged to Mary, who has told you that she is pregnant with the Son of God. Give the kids ten or fifteen minutes to work on these letters; then they can be passed in, read to the group, and discussed. The results will be very meaningful.

### LIVING CHRISTMAS GIFT

Here is a clever and meaningful Christmas gift suggestion that will become more valuable as the years go by. Have your young people interview their grandparents about their experiences in life (sort of an autobiography on tape). Suggest that the young people duplicate the tape and give a copy to each of the relatives for Christmas.

### LIVING MANGER SCENE

This can be a very effective idea for a church in the city, if city ordinances don't prohibit it. Construct a stable on the church grounds, and bring in some real animals, like a donkey and some sheep. Have your young people take shifts as Mary, Joseph, the shepherds, etc. This can be a big attraction on Christmas Eve, especially for the younger children. Provide some hay or grain so that the kids can feed the animals. This can add a little more "realism" to the Christmas story for young and old alike.

### MARY'S STORY

The following play is based on the Christmas story and is excellent for use during the holiday season. But it is perhaps even more effective when presented at a time other than Christmas to heighten the "element of surprise" at the ending. The names of the characters are not given during the play itself. The setting is modern times. Each of the scenes can be set up any way you choose, and the dialogue has been written in such a way as to allow you the freedom to change or add to it as you see fit. The play was originally written by Beverly Snedden and the youth group of Calvary Baptist Church in Kansas City, Missouri.

*Characters Needed:*

|  |  |
|---|---|
| Mary | Neighbors |
| Joseph | Elizabeth |
| Mother | The Doctor |
| Dad | The Psychiatrist |

Mary's Friends (I and II)          The Rabbi
Carpenters (I and II)              Joe's Parents
Teachers (I and II)

## Scene One (Girls sitting around a table discussing the upcoming dance)

| | |
|---|---|
| *Girl I:* | What are you going to wear? |
| *Mary:* | I don't know if I'm going. |
| *Girl II:* | Everybody's going. It'll be a good dance. |
| *Mary:* | I can't even dance. Anyway, I wouldn't know how to ask a guy for a date. |
| *Girl I:* | This is your chance to get around. |
| *Girl II:* | What about that guy your parents like? Do they still want you to marry him when you get out of school? |
| *Girl I:* | I hear he's got his own business and a sharp car. |
| *Girl II:* | The guy I'm going with has a new Corvette. |

## Scene Two (Mary kneeling beside her bed)

| | |
|---|---|
| *Mary:* | *(This can be ad-libbed somewhat.)* Why me? What am I going to tell mom and dad? . . . What will my friends think? . . . What is he going to do? . . . They're never going to believe me. . . . |

## Scene Three (The living room with Mary's parents sitting on the couch)

| | |
|---|---|
| *Mom:* | Well, I asked her what was wrong, but I wasn't able to get much out of her. She claims there's a lot of pressure from her teacher giving her a big assignment. |
| *Dad:* | Well, that doesn't sound like our little girl. She doesn't usually let something like that bother her so much. I've heard a lot about the drug problem at her school. I'm sure our daughter has been raised well enough not to do anything like that, but that doesn't mean the pressure isn't hurting her. Maybe I could talk to her. |
| *Mom:* | Well, I guess it couldn't hurt but be careful not to hurt her more. She's been awfully touchy lately. |

## Scene Four (Two girls talking on the phone)

| | |
|---|---|
| *Girl I:* | I'm worried about her. She's been acting strange lately. Crying about silly things. |
| *Girl II:* | Yeah, I've noticed. |
| *Girl I:* | Have you noticed she's gained weight? |
| *Girl II:* | Yeah, maybe it's from all that broccoli and other health food she's been eating. |
| *Girl I:* | She won't go out with us—not even to the dance we all went to. She says she's too tired. |

| Girl II: | She's had the flu a lot lately. Maybe I'll call her and see how she's feeling. |
|---|---|

## Scene Five (The teacher's lounge at school)

| Teacher I: | She's been acting differently lately. |
|---|---|
| Teacher II: | Her grades sure have dropped and she's been missing my class a lot. |
| Teacher I: | She seems lonely. She isn't around her old crowd anymore. |
| Teacher II: | She's also been putting on weight and wearing those loose tops. |
| Teacher I: | She's in my first-hour English class and she's asked to see the nurse a lot. Do you think she's in trouble? She's so sweet. |

## Scene Six (Two neighbors talking over the back fence)

| Neighbor I: | I just *know* she is! And with those wonderful parents, too . . . they've tried so hard to bring her up right. |
|---|---|
| Neighbor II: | I bet I know who the father is . . . that older boy her father knows. He's the only one I've seen at the house. |
| Neighbor I: | You never know, do you? She just didn't seem the type . . . so well behaved and respectful. |
| Neighbor II: | She goes to Synagogue every week. What is the world coming to? |

## Scene Seven (Two carpenters sawing boards)

| Carpenter I: | Poor guy . . . that's too bad. |
|---|---|
| Carpenter II: | He's got to be crazy to marry her. |
| Carpenter I: | I'd hate to be in his place. |
| Carpenter II: | Be quiet, he's coming. |

## Scene Eight (The living room. Mom and dad are talking to Mary and Joseph when three men enter.)

| Mom: | Where did I go wrong? (*Door bell rings. Father gets up to answer it and escorts in three men.*) |
|---|---|
| Father: | Gentlemen, we have discovered our daughter is pregnant and we don't know what to do. We need your expert opinions about what we should do. We don't want her life and future ruined. |
| Doctor: | As a physician, the only option I can see for a girl her age is to terminate the pregnancy. If you choose abortion, we'll have to act quickly. Then no one else will have to know. |
| Psychiatrist: | From the viewpoint of a psychiatrist, her emotional stability would probably stand an abortion better than adoption. If you choose for her to give birth to the child, she might want to keep it and I believe that would be a grave mistake. |
| Rabbi: | They must get married. I know they're young, but with prayer the marriage can work. |

| | |
|---|---|
| Father: | *(To Joseph)* You got her into this—what do you have to say? |
| Mary: | I'm going to have my baby and keep him. With the Lord's help, I can handle it. |
| Joseph: | I had considered breaking it off, but I've prayed about the situation and have decided it's God's will that we should be married. I'll do my best to be a good father to the baby. |

## Scene Nine (The living room with Mary and Elizabeth)

| | |
|---|---|
| Mary: | He wonders whether or not our marriage will work. I want it to work. |
| Elizabeth: | He's a quiet person who loves his work. I'm sure he's worried about the gossip you've told me about. |
| Mary: | Yes, I feel it's affecting our relationship. He's so practical that he can't believe how I got pregnant. No one believes him when he says he isn't the father. |
| Elizabeth: | I understand what you are going through, but we know it will be worth it. When the baby is born everything will be okay, you'll see. |
| Mary: | You're only my cousin, but you're more like a sister to me. |

## Scene Ten (Mary and Joseph)

| | |
|---|---|
| Mary: | I'm really frightened about you leaving on this trip. The doctor says that the baby could come anytime now. |
| Joseph: | Yeah, I know, but I have to go! The only solution is having you go with me. |
| Mary: | Well, I'd rather be with you when the time comes. You know, I am really excited about the baby. God has given me peace that we have done the right thing. |
| Joseph: | I really feel that way, now. We have a big job ahead of us. We first of all must be sure that we are completely dedicated to God so we can guide our little son. |

## Scene Eleven (Mary and Joseph with the new baby. The doctor, the psychiatrist, and the rabbi enter, bringing gifts for the baby. They kneel and worship Him.)

| | |
|---|---|
| Doctor: | *(To Mary and Joseph)* Forgive us, for our prejudice and judgments. We are here to give you and your son our love. |
| Psychiatrist: | Through prayer we were able to understand your situation. |
| Rabbi: | Mary, what will you name Him? |
| Mary: | He has been named . . . Jesus. |

## MYSTERY GIFTS

Wrap several mystery gifts using seasonal paper for wrapping. Vary the size of the boxes. Have several kids come up and select a "gift" from a box or pile of gifts. They should open them before the group and give an impromptu "parable," thought, or lesson with the "gift" as a theme. If the treasury can afford it, the participants may keep the gifts. This is a great way to enhance creativity at Christmas or anytime.

## PARABLE OF THE BIRDS

The following short story is effective for helping kids to better understand the Incarnation and the meaning of Christmas or to open up a Bible study on John 1:1–18. It was written by the late journalist Louis Cassels and is used here with his permission.

Once upon a time, there was a man who looked upon Christmas as a lot of humbug. He wasn't a Scrooge. He was a very kind and decent person, generous to his family, upright in all his dealings with other men. But he didn't believe all that stuff about an incarnation which churches proclaim at Christmas. And he was too honest to pretend that he did.

"I am truly sorry to distress you," he told his wife, who was a faithful churchgoer. "But I simply cannot understand this claim that God became man. It doesn't make any sense to me."

On Christmas Eve, his wife and children went to church for the midnight service. He declined an invitation to accompany them.

"I'd feel like a hypocrite," he explained. "I'd much rather stay at home. But I'll wait up for you."

Shortly after his family drove away in the car, snow began to fall. He went to the window and watched the flurries getting heavier and heavier.

"If we must have Christmas," he reflected, "it's nice to have a white one." He went back to his chair by the fireside and began to read his newspaper.

A few minutes later he was startled by a thudding sound. It was quickly followed by another, then another. He thought that someone must be throwing snowballs at his window.

When he went to the front door to investigate, he found a flock of birds huddled miserably in the snow. They had been caught in the storm and in a desperate search for shelter had tried to fly through his window.

"I can't let those poor creatures lie there and freeze," he thought, "but how can I help them?"

Then he remembered the barn where the children's pony was stabled. It would provide a warm shelter. He quickly put on his coat and galoshes and tramped through the deepening snow to the barn. He opened the doors wide and turned on the light.

But the birds didn't come in.

"Food will bring them in," he thought. So he hurried back to the house for bread crumbs, which he sprinkled on the snow to make a trail into the barn. To his dismay, the birds ignored the bread crumbs and continued to flop around helplessly in the snow.

He tried shooing them into the barn by walking around and waving his arms. They scattered in every direction . . . except into the warm, lighted barn.

"If only I could be a bird myself for a few minutes, perhaps I could lead them to safety," he thought.

Just at that moment the church bells began to ring. He stood silently for awhile, listening to the bells pealing the glad tidings of Christmas. Then he sank to his knees in the snow.

"Now I understand," he whispered. "Now I see why You had to do it."

## PERSONALIZED CHRISTMAS STORY

Have the members of the group tell their version of the Christmas story, using what they remember from the passages in Luke, Matthew, and traditional stories. Using a blackboard or poster paper, write down the key points. When they have finished, read the passages from Luke and Matthew and see how their versions compare with the Bible. The results can lead to some very effective discussion and learning.

## SANTA'S BIRTHDAY PARTY

Around Christmas time plan a birthday party for someone in the youth group (depending on the person, it might be best to clue her in as to what you are doing). Use a lot of publicity and include the fact that Santa will be appearing at the party with gifts for everyone. Each person that attends the party must bring a gift for the birthday person and one other gift.

Although the party is supposed to be a birthday party, do everything you can to emphasize Santa's appearance. Hang signs that say, "Welcome Santa," and put the Christmas tree with gifts in a central location. The "Happy Birthday" signs and cake should be small and off to the side.

At the party play some games, and then sing "Happy Birthday." While you are singing "Happy Birthday" to the birthday person, have Santa appear with surprises and distribute the extra gifts for everyone. Make a big deal out of Santa's appearance with picture taking and have the kids sit on Santa's lap.

After Santa leaves and there is a pause, then remember the birthday person and have her open the birthday gifts. At the end of the get together discuss what took place. What happened to the birthday person? How did she feel when Santa got all the attention? Would you want to be the one for whom the party was given?

## SIGHTS AND SOUNDS OF CHRISTMAS

If your youth ministry is in the city and most of the kids are "city kids," the following Christmas activity could be very meaningful. Take the youth group to a farm or ranch where there is a barn or stable, perhaps similar to the nativity setting. Allow the kids to imagine how Joseph and Mary must have felt, having to give birth to Jesus in such an environment. Perhaps a manger scene could be set up there, and each young person could symbolically offer a gift to Jesus as the wise men did. Singing Christmas carols and reading Scripture make for an effective worship experience.

## SNOWFLAKES

Have everyone cut a "snowflake" out of paper (like they did in the first grade) and write their name on it. Then using the snowflakes as examples, talk about the unique beauty of everyone in the group. Close this program by having everyone pass the snowflakes around and write an affirming statement or perhaps a Christian wish on them for the owner of that snowflake.

## TOY COLLECTION

Every town has some organization which collects toys at Christmas for needy children. A good group activity would be to have a toy drive, where the kids go door-to-door to collect old unwanted toys that are still usable or that require minor repairs. They can be repaired, if necessary, and then distributed or given to an agency who distributes them. This can be made into a contest to see which team can collect the most toys within a given time limit.

## POLAROID CHRISTMAS TREE

If your youth group has a Christmas tree, you might try this very rewarding idea. Take a picture of each person in your youth group. (If you don't have a Polaroid camera, then have the kids bring pictures of themselves.) Have them glue their picture on a small paper plate, punch a hole in the top, and put in a piece of yarn to hang the "ornament." Then have them decorate the plate with crayons, magic markers, and whatever else you can provide. On the back of the plate have the kids write down a Christmas wish. Hang the ornaments on the tree and encourage the kids to read the wishes on the other ornaments.

## TOY DISCUSSION

Christmas is a time when people buy dozens of toys for their children. As a discussion starter, have the kids in your youth group go through a toy store or a department store catalog and list toys as either "good" or "bad" for children. They should explain why they categorized the toys one way or the other. Have the kids discuss what values are taught by different kinds of toys that are on the market. Have them share feelings about their favorite toys when they were children.

## TV CHRISTMAS STORY

Here is a dramatic presentation that can be given at Christmas time centered around a television newscast. The newscast occurs on the first Christmas day but is done with a modern set. Simply reproduce a large TV news set complete with monitor, station call letters in the back, etc. You could even go so far as to construct phony cameras, etc. All of the news commentators should be dressed in modern clothes. Feel free to adapt, add to, or subtract any part of the script you want.

*Characters Needed:*

| | |
|---|---|
| Announcer | Martha Waltersberg |
| Commercial Announcer | Mort Solomon |
| Barnabas Cronkite | Eric Rosen |
| Moshe Smith | Stud Barjonas |
| David Saul | |

**Ann:** Stay tuned for the VBS Evening News with Barnabas Cronkite with the latest on a strange sighting in the sky; Martha Waltersberg from downtown Bethlehem where a huge crowd is gathering for the tax enrollment; and Dr. Ben Hadad with reports about a new cold front moving in. That's the VBS news coming up next.

**Com:** Taxes. Taxes. Taxes. No one likes to pay taxes, but H & R Blockberg can help you pay the lowest taxes possible. H & R Blockberg is the only tax consulting service authorized by the Roman government, *and* each and every consultant has previous tax collecting experience. Yes, you can trust H & R Blockberg for all your tax-related problems. H & R Blockberg, 700 Appian Way.

**Ann:** The VBS Evening News with Barnabas Cronkite in Jerusalem, Martha Waltersberg in Bethlehem, and Dr. Ben Hadad on Mt. Ararat. Brought to you by Hertz Donkey Rental—the donkeys O. J. Feldman rides and by Gethsemane Nurseries, with gardens in every major city. Now . . . Barnabas Cronkite.

**Bar:** Good Evening. There has been a new development on the strange light that has been sighted in the eastern hemisphere for the last few nights. Correspondent Moshe Smith reports.

**Mos:** For the past few nights a bright light or starlike phenomena has been appearing in the sky. At first it was thought to be a meteor or an optical illusion, but tonight Dr. Ishmael Streisand confirmed that what everyone is seeing is, in fact, a star. The question is, Where did this star come from and what does it mean. Officials close to the situation are speculating that the star is not an isolated incident and that more strange occurrences may be expected. Concerned government officials are monitoring the situation closely, and reliable sources have told VBS that other similar incidents have not been made public. This is Correspondent Moshe Smith in Jerusalem.

**Bar:** VBS news has learned that an incident did occur near Bethlehem and we now switch to our mini-cam live in the hills of Bethlehem. David Saul reports.

**Dav:** Barnabas, approximately ten minutes ago a group of shepherds told me that they saw some kind of an angel accompanied by music and bright lights. Normally, stories from shepherds are discounted because of the fact that they are a strange breed . . . and tend to hit the sauce . . . *but* government officials here seem strangely concerned. From my discussions with the shepherds, apparently they think this has something to do with a Messiah promised years ago. The mention of the Messiah seems to have government officials concerned. From the hills of Bethlehem, this has been David Saul reporting.

**Bar:** We'll be right back after this message from Hertz.

**Com:** O. J. Feldman here for Hertz. When you're in a strange town, it's nice to know your friends at Hertz are ready to help. Maybe you had to trade in your donkey for tax money, or maybe yours kicks people in crowds. That's the time to rent a donkey from Hertz. Our donkeys are used to crowds and are guaranteed to get you where you want to go. Of course, Hertz uses nothing but fine GMAC donkeys. Hertz—where we treat donkeys like donkeys and treat you right.

**Bar:** Last month Caesar Augustus issued a decree requiring all citizens to return to their city of birth in order to attain an accurate enrollment for taxing. Martha Waltersberg is in Bethlehem for the story.

Mar: I'm standing here at the No Room Inn on the outskirts of Bethlehem. Thousands of people are swarming into the city now and every available facility is full. Just a few minutes ago a woman who is about to have a baby was almost turned away. Finally, after protests from her husband, they were allowed to stay with the animals. We just finished talking with the head of the Best Eastern Lodge Association, and he suggests that anyone heading for Bethlehem attempt to find lodging outside of town. The head of the Roman government here in Bethlehem is deeply concerned about crowd control. So far there have not been any major incidents. The question is, can this uneasy quiet continue? Martha Waltersberg at the No Room Inn in Bethlehem.

Bar: A group of highly respected astrologers have begun a significant journey. Correspondent Mort Solomon reports from Peking.

Mor: Walter, a large party of wealthy astrologers are traveling towards Israel to observe a strange light. Apparently it is the same strange light seen over Israel during the past few weeks. Informed sources have told us that these men believe there is some relation between the light and the Messiah. Although there has been no official recognition by the Roman government, it is believed that when the astrologers arrive within Roman territory they will be summoned before government officials. Reporters here, Walter, are baffled as to this sudden concern on the part of Roman officials for this promised Messiah. Why, we just will have to wait and see. Mort Solomon from China.

Com: The VBS news will continue in just a moment. Ladies, now is the time to order your hooded capes and robes. The Good Hood Company has an incredible selection now. These hooded capes and robes are all one piece of material so the hood cannot be lost nor can it become entangled in water jugs being carried on the head. The Good Hood Company—where we also have a clearance on beautiful sheepskin swimming suits. Come by and see us soon.

Bar: Eric Rosen has been watching with interest the increasing speculation about a coming Messiah. Eric.

Eric: The reason there is so much concern about a Messiah, of course, is the popular notion by the Jews that such a Messiah will become a political force and overthrow the Romans. This is a hope that Jews have had for years, and we have seen potential "Messiahs" come and go. We have a feeling that the strange light in the East is nothing more than a passing phenomena that those who are overly religious and mystical can cling to, or, worse yet, use to mount a revolutionary movement. I have done some research on this matter of a Messiah and I am not so sure that if and when such a Savior were to appear, He would be a political leader. I am sure I will get a lot of mail about this, but I think it would be much more profitable if those who are so anxiously awaiting a Messiah would start living as if they believed in the God they say they believe in. I guess it is always easier and less threatening to hope in the future than to live as if the future were now. Eric Rosen. VBS news.

Bar: Jerusalem has been the home of the National Open Spear Throwing Olympics. Stud Barjonas reports.

Stud: Coming from major upset victories, two Hebrews will be facing each other in the finals to be held next Friday. Friday's match between Philip of Caesarea and

152

Simion of Bethany has already been sold out. There is some concern that Philip of Caesarea may have trouble keeping his feet within the specified boundaries on his approach. He refused comment on the two warnings he received today. However, sources close to Philip confirm that he will be wearing a new imported brand of sandal to give him additional footing. Should be quite a match. In chariot racing today, Fireball Jonah narrowly escaped serious injury when his vehicle turned over in the northwest turn at the Hippodrome. This turn is considered one of the most hazardous in racing. In spite of the mishap, Jonah went on to win the main event.

Bar: Dr. Ben Hadad has been standing by on Mt. Ararat for the weather report, but we have just received a bulletin from Bethlehem. Martha Waltersberg is there.

Mar: Walter, as you know from my earlier report, I am at the No Room Inn here in Bethlehem. Just as we were getting ready to leave, we were told of a commotion at the back of the inn. We found a young girl who had just given birth to a baby in the stable where they keep the animals. Normally, we would have ignored the story, but, Walter, something strange is occurring here. A huge crowd is gathering and a number of shepherds and others almost seem to be worshipping the baby. We have been unable to get any comment from anyone here, but there is one thing else. That strange light in the East seems to be much brighter now and almost seems to be directly above us. This is Martha Waltersberg in a stable in Bethlehem.

Bar: And that's the way it is. Barnabas Cronkite for the VBS Evening News. Good night.

# Other Holidays

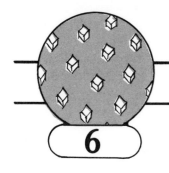

# Other Holidays

## 6

## April Fools' Day

### APRIL FOOLS' GAME

At the beginning of a party or special event, give everyone in the room a card with an instruction written on it. The instruction should be an April Fools' trick that he must play on someone before the event is over. For example, it might say, "Tell someone that his fly is open," or "Tell someone that there is a phone call for him," and so on. If the person falls for it (looks down, goes to get the phone, etc.), then that person has been officially "fooled" and is out of the game. The idea is to try and avoid being fooled and to eliminate as many others as you possibly can by faking them out. This works best when there is plenty of time and while other things are going on as well. Check at the end of the party or event how many people were fooled, who fooled the most people, and so on. It's fun!

### OTHER APRIL FOOLS' GAMES

There is an old game in which you ask for volunteers to compete in a kind of speech contest. They must leave the room with a leader who explains to them what they are going to do. They are told that they will be given a chance to "practice" while out of the room. The audience should then be clued in. When the volunteers return, one at a time, they are to try and see how many times they can say, "What am I doing" in fifteen seconds. They must say it over and over as fast as they possibly can. They should be told that the winner will receive an incredible prize. Then when they do it, the crowd should answer back in unison, "Making a big fool out of yourself!"

This is generally referred to as a "fall guy" routine in which someone has a joke played on him or her that provides a lot of laughs for everyone (hopefully including the "fall guy"). There are hundreds of these kinds of stunts like "Buzz, Buzz, Little Bee," "The Funnel Trick," "The Submarine Ride," "First Kiss," and others. They can be found in the book *Fun 'N' Games* by Rice, Rydberg, and Yaconelli (Zondervan) or in the *Ideas* books, published by Youth Specialties, 1224 Greenfield Drive, El Cajon, California 92021. By using a few of these, you can design a hilarious evening of games and stunts for April Fools' Day that will be remembered for a long time.

# Back to School/Graduation

## CRAZY COLLEGE ENTRANCE EXAMS

The following "tests of intelligence" can be used either at the beginning or the end of the school year. The first one is a list of twenty questions that are fun to try and figure out. The person with the most incorrect answers gets to wear the "dunce" hat.

1. If you went to bed at 8 o'clock a.m. and set the alarm to get up at 9 o'clock the next morning, how many hours of sleep would you get? _____

2. Does England have a Fourth of July? _____

3. Why can't a man living in Winston-Salem, North Carolina, be buried west of the Mississippi River? _____

4. If you had a match and entered a room in which there were a kerosene lamp, an oil heater, and a wood-burning stove, which would you light first? _____

5. Some months have 30 days, some have 31 days. How many months have 28 days?

6. A man builds a house with four sides to it and it is rectangular in shape. Each side has a southern exposure. A big bear came wandering by, what color is the bear? _____

7. How far can a dog run into the woods? _____

8. What four words appear on every denomination of U.S. coin? _____

9. What is the minimum of baseball players on the field during any part of an inning in a regular game? _____ How many outs in an inning? _____

10. I have in my hand two U.S. coins which total 55 cents in value. One is not a nickel. What are the two coins? _____

11. A farmer had 17 sheep; all but nine died. How many does he have left? _____

12. Divide 30 by one-half and add 10. What is the answer? _____

13. Take two apples from three apples and what do you have? _____

14. An archaeologist claimed he found some gold coins dated 46 B.C. Do you think he did? _____ Explain: _____

15. A woman gives a beggar 50 cents. The woman is the beggar's sister but the beggar is not the woman's brother. How come? _____

16. How many animals of each species did Moses take aboard the ark with him? _____

17. Is it legal in North Carolina for a man to marry his widow's sister? _____ Why?

18. What word in this test is mispelled? _____

19. From what animal do we get whale bones? _____

20. Where was Paul going on the road to Damascus? _____

**Answers:**

1. One hour
2. Yes
3. Because he's not dead
4. The match
5. They all do
6. White
7. Halfway. The other half, he's running *out*
8. "United States of America" or "In God We Trust"
9. Ten—nine fielders and a batter; six outs per inning
10. 50¢ and 5¢. One is not a nickel but the other is.
11. Nine
12. Seventy
13. Two
14. No. The dating system didn't exist until after Christ was born.

| | |
|---|---|
| 15. They are sisters | 18. Misspelled |
| 16. None. *Noah* took the animals, not Moses | 19. Whale |
| 17. No. He is dead | 20. Damascus |

For this one, the object of the test is to follow directions. Tell the group that it is a timed test, and they must complete the entire test in only two minutes. Pass out the test to the kids and have them keep them face down until you say "start." The results are usually a lot of fun.

## LEADERSHIP ACHIEVEMENT TEST

Directions: Answer each question in sequence. If you do not know an answer, go on to the next one. Read through entire test before starting on question number one.

1. Print complete name in upper left hand corner.

2. Print address _____

3. Underline the correct answer:

   A. A good leader must be: Dogmatic, Restrictive, Dedicated

   B. The best kind of leadership is: Authoritative, Socialist, Democratic

   C. The best way to get something done is: Form a committee, Do it yourself, Have others do it

4. Put your age in the upper right hand corner.

5. Raise your left hand until recognized by the instructor.

6. True or False: (circle correct answer)

   A. A good leader always has an answer. It is a sign of weakness not to have an answer. T  F

   B. A good leader should know how to follow directions. T  F

   C. A good leader gets things done fast. T  F

   D. It is better to do a job right rather than to do it quickly. T  F

7. In question 6-B, underline the words "follow directions."

8. Stand up until recognized.

9. Define a leader (approximately 50 words) on the back of this page.

10. If you have read through this entire test as you were instructed to do, you don't have to take it. Just sign your name in the upper right hand corner and wait until the time is up. Do not answer questions 1 through 9.

The next test involves combinations of letters and numbers that represent by their arrangement common phrases or sayings. The object is to decipher each one.

1. | SAND |

2. _MAN_
   BOARD

3. _STAND_
   I

4. R|E|A|D|I|N|G

5. _WEAR_
   LONG

6. R
   ROAD
    A
    D

7. CYCLE
   CYCLE
   CYCLE

8. T
   O
   W
   N

9. LE$_{VEL}$

10. KNEE
    LIGHT

11. **CHAIR**

12. DICE  DICE

13. T
    O
    U
    C
    H

14. GROUND
      FEET
      FEET
      FEET
      FEET
      FEET
      FEET

15. _MIND_
    MATTER

16. HE'S/HIMSELF

160

17. ECNALG

18.

19. † †

20. K
C
E
H
C

21. 0–144

22. OFF

23. SIDE/SIDE

24.   L
KYOUO
   O

25. DOCTOR
DOCTOR

26. DATE
DATE

27. GIRL FELLOW FELLOW

28. L E G A L

29. GIRL $1,000,000

30. FAR       HOME

31. GNIKOOL

32. <u>MONEY</u>

33. SUN., MON., TUES.,
THURS., FRI., SAT.

34. R R R R R R R
R R R R R R R
R R R R R R R
R R R R R R R
R R R R R R R
R R R R R R R
R R R R R R R

35. A L L O

36. 2th DK

37.   0
D.D.S.
LL.D
PH.D
M.A.
M.D.

38. OUT
    3 2 1

39. RE  RE

40. EVERY RIGHT THING

41. F FAR E FAR W

42. 1  1

43. EZ
    i i

44.  YOUR HAT
     KEEP IT

45. EVERYTHING

46. WETHER

47. WORL

48. BANGFF

49. BRILLIANT SURGEON
    BRILLIANT SURGEON

50.   N
        E
          W
      THINGS

51. WOWOLFOL

52. SSSSSSSSSSC

53. S H I P

**Answers:**

1. Sandbox
2. Man overboard
3. I understand
4. Reading between the lines
5. Long underwear
6. Road crossing
7. Tricycle
8. Downtown
9. Split level
10. Neon light
11. High chair
12. Paradise
13. Touchdown
14. Six feet under ground
15. Mind over matter
16. He's beside himself
17. Backward glance
18. See-through blouse
19. Double cross
20. Check up
21. Oh gross!
22. Cut off
23. Side by side
24. Look around you
25. Paradox
26. Double date
27. Two fellows after the same girl
28. Legal separation
29. Girl with a million-dollar figure
30. Far away from home
31. Looking backward
32. Money on the line
33. A week with one day off
34. Forty-niners
35. Nothing after all
36. Tooth decay
37. Five degrees below zero
38. Outnumbered three to one
39. Repaired
40. Right between everything
41. Few and far between
42. One after another
43. Easy on the eyes
44. Keep it under your hat
45. Everything's going up
46. Bad spell of weather
47. World without end
48. Starting off with a bang
49. A couple of sharp operators
50. A new slant on things
51. Wolf in sheep's clothing
52. Tennessee
53. Space ship

## SCHOOL'S OUT

As the last week of school approaches, help your kids celebrate their freedom from the clutches of education by having a "burn, baby, burn" night. Encourage the kids to bring their old notebooks, tests, and papers that they would like to burn. Throw it all in one pile and have a bonfire. You'll be surprised how much paper those kids will bring. Note: Make sure kids don't burn anything that they might wish they had someday.

## GRADUATION SUNDAY POSTER

It's time-honored tradition in most churches to recognize the graduating class one Sunday in May or June of each year, but here's a way to make it a bit more meaningful to everyone. Print up a poster that features the senior pictures of each person who is graduating. It can also include information regarding each graduate's college or employment plans as well. Make sure you have it printed by a good offset printer so that the pictures are clear. It's not that expensive. Besides adding a little prestige to the whole thing (which the graduates really appreciate), it helps people to get to know their graduates a little better. The posters can also be hung in people's homes as a reminder to pray for the graduates. Graduation really is a big deal for most kids, and things like this let them know the church is proud of them.

## SUPERLATIVES

Have your youth group vote on some "Most Likely to . . ." awards at the end of each school year or at summer camp, etc., only make them really ridiculous. You can have an awards ceremony and perhaps honor a "king" and "queen"—people who got the most nominations. They can get the "royal" treatment and be brought in on a presidential limo (wheelbarrow) and so on. Make up your own categories, but here are a few suggestions:

1. Most likely to burst out laughing at his/her wedding. _____
2. Most likely to tattoo one of his/her siblings. _____
3. Most likely to have a complete set of C.S. Lewis books by the toilet in the bathroom. _____
4. Biggest flirt in town award. _____
5. Most likely to move his/her lips to fake singing during church. _____
6. Most likely to pick his/her nose in private. _____
7. Most likely to name his/her child something like Elvis, Pope John Paul, Festus, or Elrod. _____
8. Most likely to still care if Spider Man makes it out of a jam when he/she is eighty years old. _____
9. Most likely to spill his/her milk at lunch. _____
10. Most likely to cry when he/she makes an "A-" on a test. _____

11. Most likely to talk in his/her sleep in church. _____
12. Most likely to always act like a seventh grader. _____
13. Most likely to feed his/her children granola bars for breakfast. _____
14. Most likely to try to borrow money from you. _____
15. Most likely to have his/her driver's license revoked. _____
16. Most likely to go through life missing the point of most jokes. _____
17. Most likely to bite his/her toenails. _____
18. Most likely to use the "we had a flat tire" excuse on his/her parents.
_____
19. Most likely to wear his/her underwear inside out. _____
20. Most likely to have the coat hangers in his/her closet all going the same direction.
_____
21. Most likely to be disappointed if he/she doesn't become famous. _____
22. Most likely to act dumb and actually be smart. _____
23. Most likely to act smart and actually be dumb. _____
24. Most likely to purposely step on cracks in the concrete. _____
25. Most likely to never remember one Sunday school lesson. _____
26. Most likely to wear pajamas on campouts. _____
27. Most likely to talk about the same thing all the time. _____
28. Most likely to force his/her children to eat liver, squash, spinach, and such.
_____
29. Most likely to examine ear wax under a microscope while taking biology.
_____
30. Most likely to dress like a fifteen-year-old at the age of fifty. _____
31. Most likely to write an autobiography. _____
32. Most likely to wear a Purina checkerboard plaid sportcoat. _____
33. Most likely to inevitably not hear the correct page number of hymns when announced
in church. _____
34. Most likely to steal jokes all his/her life and fake like they are originals.
_____
35. Most likely to think he/she is too old for youth meetings in the eighth grade.
_____

## TEN YEARS FROM NOW

This is a good discussion starter that would be appropriate for a graduation night celebration. Print the questions below on a half sheet of paper and let the kids write in their answers. Let everyone participate, not just the graduates. Then you might divide the group into small discussion groups of four or five per group and let the kids share their answers with the others.

```
┌─────────────────────────────────────────────────────┐
│              TEN YEARS FROM NOW . . .                 │
│                                                       │
│        1. My height                                   │
│        2. My weight                                   │
│        3. My hair style                               │
│        4. Where I will be living                      │
│        5. What I will be doing                        │
│        6. Dreams and goals I will have                │
│        7. I FEEL I WILL HAVE BEEN A SUCCESS IN LIFE IF . . . │
│                                                       │
│        8. I WILL LOOK BACK UPON THIS YEAR AS A YEAR OF . . . │
│                                                       │
└─────────────────────────────────────────────────────┘
```

## THE TWELVE DAYS OF SCHOOL

Here's a fun song that the group can sing, or that you can do as a skit with one person taking each line and acting out each part. It should be sung to the same tune as the "Twelve Days of Christmas."

"On the first day of school, my mommy said to me . . ."

*First day:* "Don't ever wet your pants."
*Second day:* "Don't lift your dress."
*Third day:* "Don't eat your crayons."
*Fourth Day:* "Don't chew gum."
*Fifth Day:* "Don't pick your nose."
*Sixth day:* "Don't hold hands."
*Seventh day:* "Don't throw spitballs."
*Eighth day:* "Don't ever belch."
*Ninth day:* "Don't sleep in class."
*Tenth day:* "Don't be a sissy."
*Eleventh day:* "Don't bite your toenails."
*Twelfth day:* "Don't kiss the girls (boys)."

# Columbus Day

## CHRISTOPHER COLUMBUS

Here's a great skit for Columbus Day. It requires only two people, the reporter, and Columbus. Lines should be memorized for best results.

*Reporter:* (Holding microphone) This is Camron-camron Holmes, coming to you from the ship Santa Maria, far out in the unknown sea. The year is 1483. We're waiting to see if we can get an interview with the famed Christopher Columbus.

*Columbus:* (Talking to the men of his ship) Come on men, let's get this ship moving faster. Pull up another sail! Quit that sleeping on deck and get to your duties. We've got to discover the new world. I know you're cold and hungry. This voyage is a hardship for all of us, but think of the adventure of it and the great service you'll be doing for mankind by proving the world is round. You are all great sailors, men, and you and our ship will never be forgotten because we set forth with courage and faith to discover the new world.

*Reporter:* Excuse me, Admiral Columbus. Could I have a word with you?

*Columbus:* *(Still talking to men)* Yes, men, the first to see the new world. Think of that! No longer will you be prisoners in the dungeons of Spain, but notable men of the sea.

*Reporter:* Excuse me, Admiral Columbus. Could I have a word with you?

*Columbus:* Oh, pardon me young man. I didn't know you were around.

*Reporter:* Columbus, you were really giving an enthusiastic challenge to your sailors on this long trip. How long have you been out to sea?

*Columbus:* Fifteen minutes.

*Reporter:* I see. Columbus, how do you handle being away from home, out on the ocean, for such a long period of time. After all, it's a long way to the new world.

*Columbus:* Well, it's because I love the sea. And I love this ship. I'm married to this ship, mister, and that's the finest wife a man could ever have!

*Reporter:* That's very romantic. Oh, by the way, what are those other two ships following along behind?

*Columbus:* Those are the kids. We call them Pinta and Nina. Cute little rascals, aren't they? They take after their mother.

*Reporter:* Columbus, what compels a man of your character to set sail for the purpose of discovering the new world?

*Columbus:* It's because I like poetry. I write poetry you see. I'm not much concerned about what I discover. I just want a poem.

*Reporter:* What kind of a poem do you want?

*Columbus:* Oh, just a simple little poem about me. You know . . . one all the school kids could learn and remember my name by. I've been doing some writing. Listen to this. "In fourteen hundred and eighty-three, Columbus sailed as fast as a bee." I know it's not real good, but it's a start. Do you have any suggestions?

*Reporter:* Well . . . what about this "In fourteen hundred and eighty-three, Beneath the swaying chestnut tree."

*Columbus:* Yea, that's the idea. I like that very much, but you *left out my name.* Here's another. "In fourteen hundred and eighty-three, Columbus exhibited his gallantry." That's still not it, but it's got to ring something like that.

*Reporter:* Yea, I see what you mean. What about this one, "In fourteen hundred and eighty-three, upon the ship, upon the sea, in the midst of the storm—always courageous was our sailor, never forlorn."

*Columbus:* That's it! That's great! *(Pause)* But you *left my name out again!* Now here's another one. It has all the essentials. "In fourteen hundred and eighty-three,

Columbus is the boy for me." It's still not exactly what I want, but that's the idea.

*Reporter:* How about this. "In fourteen hundred and ninety-two, Columbus sailed the ocean blue."

*Columbus:* That's it! That's it! That's *exactly* what I've been looking for!

*Reporter:* But Columbus, 1492 is nine years from now.

*Columbus:* Who cares! All I want is a poem. *(To men on ship)* OK men, we're turning back. Turn this ship back toward Spain. We'll come back in *nine* years!

## BUCKET BRIGADE

Divide into three teams: the "Pintas," the "Ninas," and the "Santa Marias." Each team should line up single file with a bucket of water (or any water source) on one end of the line and an empty bucket on the other. Each team member (deckhand) should have a paper cup. The object of the game is to transfer the water from one bucket to the other by pouring the water from cup to cup down the line. The last team to completely fill the empty bucket with water is declared "sunk."

## COLUMBUS DAY DISCUSSION

Since Columbus is known for his great discovery of America, lead the group in a discussion on the general topic of "discoveries." Some sample questions:

1. What (in your opinion) is the greatest discovery that man has ever made?
2. What (in your opinion) is the greatest thing that man still needs to discover?
3. What is the greatest discovery that you have ever made?
4. What is the best way to go about making an important discovery?

## DISCOVERING THE NEW WORLD

A great idea for Columbus Day would be to have a treasure hunt (see the "Witch Hunt" in the Halloween chapter) in which the "treasure" would be a place that is designated as the "New World." Divide up into teams and solve clues that eventually lead to this mystery place (kept a secret), where you can then have a party. At the "New World" the hosts can dress up like Indians and welcome the explorers who have arrived. A little creativity could make this a very successful event.

## MY SHIP SAILS

Have everyone sit around on the floor (or in chairs). The leader should begin the game by taking a towel with a knot in it or a ball, and by saying, "My ship sails with . . . (and names something that begins with his initials)." For example, if his name is John Doe, he would say, "My ship sails with juicy donuts" (or jumping ducks, jolly doctors, etc.). He must then throw the towel or ball to another player in the room (who may not know how to play), and he too must say, "My ship sails with. . . ." If he knows how to play, he will say something that begins with his initials. If he doesn't know how to play, he will probably say something that does not begin with his initials and he must stand up. He must remain standing until he catches on and somebody throws the towel to him so that he gets another try. When he gets it right, he gets to sit down. The idea of this game is to see how long it takes people to catch on to what their ship sails with. To start the game, at least two or three people need to know how to play. You can explain at the beginning that not everybody's ship sails with the same thing, and the object is to discover by listening to those who know what their ship sails with, what the secret is.

## POOPDECK

Here's a great game for ten to one hundred. Play in a fairly large room or outside. Clearly mark off three sections on the floor with tape, chalk, etc. One section will be the "poopdeck," one the "maindeck," and the last the "quarter deck." Begin with everyone standing in the poopdeck area. Call out the name of a deck (even the one that they are standing in), and the kids should then run to the deck or section that you have called out. The last person into the section which you have called is out. If the kids are in "poopdeck," for example, and you call out "poopdeck," any kid who crosses the line, jumps the gun, or in any other way (except being pushed) goes out of poopdeck, is out. The game should continue rapidly until one person becomes the winner.

| POOPDECK | MAINDECK | QUARTERDECK |
| --- | --- | --- |

Other hints on playing this game: Give them a few trial runs to warm up and for new kids to get the hang of the game. Then call the decks loudly and distinctly, and to really frustrate them, point to a deck other than the one you call.

## SAILING TO AMERICA

This is a game that is fun and requires great concentration. The leader should start by saying, "I'm sailing to America, and I'm taking _____." Any word can be inserted into the blank so long as it is only one word. The second person must repeat the sentence and add one item to the list. The third person must add another, and the game continues as long as the list is repeated correctly in order. If a person forgets an item or gets items out of order, he or she is eliminated. It is best to sit in a circle and to keep going round and round until only one person is left, or until everyone gets tired of playing.

169

**ALLEGIANCE**

This is a "table-top" discussion game which requires the construction of the game board (about 24 x 36 inches on cardboard) and the discussion cards shown below.

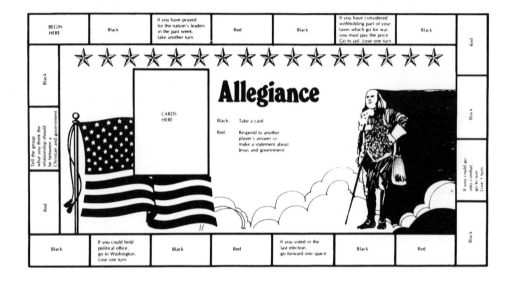

The object of Allegiance is to get the players to examine the teachings of Jesus concerning the state and related topics in light of American government and individual attitudes. The only winner is the one who responds honestly and attempts to apply the teachings of Jesus and their consequences.

Each player rolls dice to determine the amount of spaces he moves his marker (any small object) around the board. He then responds according to the space he lands on:

    a. On a black space the player takes a card and responds to the question written on it.

    b. On a red space he may respond to another player's response or make a comment concerning Jesus and government.

    c. On the other squares, the player moves as directed. (Note: the losing or gaining of a turn does not imply judgment concerning that issue, but is merely meant to add variety.)

Players may go around the board as many times as time and interest allow. Sample discussion questions for the cards are printed below:

1. Does "Render unto Caesar" include military service?
2. Could you have been a tax collector for Rome? Why or why not? (Luke 19:2–10)
3. Would you be willing to go to jail because your convictions were not compatible with the government? (Matt. 5:10)
4. Is politics a legitimate means of achieving the goals of the kingdom of heaven? (Matt. 11:12)
5. Was Jesus a "politician" in any sense of the word?
6. Name something you could *not* render unto "Caesar" (i.e. the government).
7. Would you consider Jesus an anarchist? Why or why not? (Luke 23:2)
8. Is withholding part of your taxes because of your convictions legitimate?
9. How is a servant greater than a king? (Matt. 20:25–28)
10. Name three figures of authority over you. Which are by your choice?
11. Do you believe in amnesty? How does that relate to forgiveness? (Matt. 18:21–35)
12. Could you as a Christian hold a political office? Why or why not?
13. Should you as a Christian take a stand against corruption and hypocrisy in high places? (Luke 13:32; Matt. 23:27–28)
14. Would you consider Jesus to be civilly disobedient? Why or why not? (John 9:13–16)
15. Is civil disobedience legitimate for a Christian?
16. To what extent is the public responsible for oppression, brutality, and expediency in government? How can the Christian respond?

## BATTLE OF BUNKER HILL

Arm two teams with water balloons and separate them with a line of demarcation of some kind. Each team must stay on its own side of the center line. Make boundary lines that keep both teams inside a certain field of play. The size and shape of the playing area can be up to your own discretion.

The basic idea is to try and eliminate the other team by hitting them with water balloons. Anyone who is hit with a water balloon (whether it breaks on them or not) is out of the game. However, if someone can catch a water balloon (without it breaking), whoever threw it is dead and out of the game. One team can be the Colonial army, and the other can be the British army. Set a time limit or restrict the number of balloons each side gets to determine the winner.

## FREEDOM FOR ALL

Here's a fun way to open a discussion on the topic of freedom. Divide the group into smaller groups and have each group come up with a short skit which would show what they would do if they were completely free to do their own thing with no restrictions. Then have them present the skits to the group. Most will be very funny, showing such things as; telling off their parents or teachers, dropping out of school, living it up, traveling, and so on. Surprisingly enough, these skits actually help the kids to see the chaos and futility of complete freedom. The following questions can then be used for an in-depth discussion of the topic:

1. What does the word "freedom" mean to you?
2. If you were "completely free," what would you do?
3. If *everyone* were completely free and did their own thing, what would be the result?
4. Discuss Romans 6:16–23 and Paul's concept of man as a slave.
5. Discuss Romans 7:21–25. What was Paul's problem and where did he find freedom from it?
6. How does Christ define freedom? (See John 8:31–34.)
7. Discuss freedom vs. responsibility. (See Galatians 5:13.)

## BLOW-UP ANNOUNCEMENT

Here's a clever handout idea that would be appropriate for advertising a July 4th event. Print up a card which folds in half (like a greeting card). On the front of the card print this message:

Inside the card, tape a balloon and print your announcement.

## IDENTIFY THE STATES

A simple game that would be appropriate for a Fourth of July event would be to give individuals or teams a "quiz" of some sort in which they have to identify states just by looking at the shape of the state. You could print up game sheets with the states outlined on the sheets (each should be alone, not next to adjacent states), or you could put them on an overhead projector. If you play this game with teams, one good

172

way to do it would be to flash the state up on the screen and have each team try to guess the state. As soon as they know, they should write it down on a slip of paper, hand it to a "runner" on their team, and deliver it to the "referee" at the other end of the room. The first team with the correct answer in the referee's hand is the winner.

## PAUL REVERE'S RIDE

This is a relay in which each team is divided in half, with each half of the team lined up opposite the other.

```
O O O O O O ———————→ TEAM 1 ←——————— O O O O O O
X X X X X X ———————→ TEAM 2 ←——————— X X X X X X
```

The first person in line should be given a broomstick and a hat (like Paul Revere's hat, if possible). On go, he must ride the broomstick like a horse across the playing field to his teammate on the opposite side of the field while yelling, "The British are Coming!" the entire way. The broomstick can then be passed to that player who must do the same thing back in the other direction. The first team to have all of its members make "Paul Revere's Ride" is the winner.

## REVOLUTIONARY WAR

There are a number of games that you can use for a Fourth of July event simply by calling them "Revolutionary War." The best type of game for this would involve two teams and the elimination of one of the teams in some way. There are many games like this in our book, *Fun 'N' Games,* also published by Zondervan. Examples might include; "Wells Fargo," "World War," "Balloon Stomp," "King of the Circle," and so on. Here's your chance to be creative.

## YANKEE DOODLE

Here's a crazy little game that is a lot of fun. Two people should be selected, and each should be given a lighted candle. They must stand across from each other at opposite sides of the room or as far apart as possible. The rule of the game is that neither is allowed to laugh or even smile. On "go," the two players must walk slowly toward each other, looking each other directly in the eye at all times (that's another rule). When they reach each other in the middle of the room, person number one must lift his or her hand and the following dialogue should take place:

> Person #1: "Yankee Doodle, the king of Hunky-Bunky, is defunct and dead."
> Person #2: "Alas, alas, how died he?"
> Person #1: "Just so, just so, just so."
> Person #2: "How sad, how sad, how sad."

Obviously, it will be tough for anyone to get through such a ridiculous conversation without cracking up. Give a prize to the first couple who does it successfully.

# Groundhog Day

## GROUNDHOG BANQUET

Do something really different this year and put on a "Groundhog Banquet" on Groundhog Day (February 2). If you make a big deal out of it, it will generate a lot of interest and excitement. By writing the Chamber of Commerce in Punxsutawney, Pennsylvania (where Groundhog Day originated), you can have them send you some colorful brochures that tell all about the history of Groundhog Day. You can also get souvenir groundhog statues, glasses, notepaper, decals, pennants, and all kinds of good groundhog things from them. The address is 123 S. Gilpin, Punxsutawney, PA 15767. Phone: (814) 938-7700.

For your banquet, you can call the various dishes things like; "Groundhog Stew," "Groundhog Pie," and so on. You could have a "shadow casting" contest by having contestants try to create the most interesting shadow against the wall (you could use a slide projector for light). You could play some games with groundhog names: "Groundhog Relay," "Catch the Groundhog," and so on. And you could sing some Groundhog carols like those below. With a little creativity, this could be the highlight of the year!

### I'M DREAMING OF THE GREAT GROUNDHOG

I'm dreaming of the Great Groundhog
Just like I do this time each year.
When he brings nice weather
And brings us together
To wait for him to appear.

I'm dreaming of the Great Groundhog
With every Groundhog card I write.
May your Groundhog's Day be bright
When the Great Groundhog visits you
   tonight.

### GROUNDHOG WONDERLAND

Groundhogs hoot, are you listening?
'Neath the sun, all is glist'ning
A real warm sight, we're happy tonight
Waitin' in a Groundhog wonderland.

In the field, we're watching for the
   Groundhog.
We've been waiting for this day all year.
Do you think that he will see his shadow?
And will we know if springtime's almost
   here?

Later on, while we're eating
What we got on Groundhog's Day
We'll share all our sacks
Of good Groundhog snacks
Waitin' in a Groundhog wonderland.

### DECK THE FIELD

Deck the field with brown and black
Fa la la la la la la la la.
Take along your goody sack
Fa la la la la la la la la.
Don we now our groundhog apparel
Fa la la la la la la la la
Toll the ancient groundhog carol
Fa la la la la la la la la.

See the groundhog rise before us
Fa la la la la la la la la.
As we sing the groundhog chorus
Fa la la la la la la la la.
Follow him as he ascends
Fa la la la la la la la la.
Join with true great groundhog friends
Fa la la la la la la la la.

# Labor Day

## LABOR GAME

Here is a simulation game that is good for a meeting on or near Labor Day. It is based on the parable of the laborers in the vineyard (Matthew 20:1–16). This sometimes perplexing parable can become real by allowing your youth to experience the frustration of the workers that complained about equal distribution of pay at the end of the day, even though all did not work as long or as hard. The owner (God) was just and kept His promise—paying exactly what He said He would. This would have satisfied the workers until greed crept in. The following simulation game will help kids to understand this parable more fully.

As the kids enter the room, have several tables prepared with a puzzle, a brainteaser, or a skill to do on each one. Some should be very easy, others impossible. Assign points for each puzzle, depending on the difficulty, and each person should keep track of his own score. After twenty or thirty minutes call a stop. Go to each young person, ask how many points he has, and then reach into a bag and give him a prize. The prize can be very small, just be sure every prize is exactly the same for everyone in the group.

As you slowly do this, it will soon be obvious to everyone in the group what is happening. No matter how high or low the score they tell you, they will all be receiving equal payment. Allow free talk as you distribute the reward. Follow this by discussion, prodding with questions such as "How do you honestly feel?" and "What is your attitude toward the prize-giver?" and "How do you feel toward the other young people?" Ask the one that scored the highest and the one that scored the lowest how they feel. Follow by reading the Scripture account of the parable. Discuss greed, envy, lust, and competition, and how these things can foul up one's relationship with God.

# Mother's/Father's Day

## LOOKING BACK AT PARENTS

Have the kids pick out a few adults in the church that they really respect and like a lot. It could even be their own parents. Then ask those adults (in advance) to come to the youth group meeting and share in five minutes or less what *their* parents did right. They should tell the kids what things their parents did that really helped them in their development and led them in the right way. It could be very enlightening for the kids and might help them to better understand some of the things that their own parents do.

## MOTHER'S–FATHER'S DAY BANQUET

Figure out which day falls exactly between Mother's Day and Father's Day and set aside that day to hold a Mother's-Father's Day Banquet. That's the essence of the idea, and the rest is pretty much up to you. It should be a banquet honoring parents. The kids can put it on, provide the food at their own expense, serve the meal, and provide entertainment. The parents will love it.

## MOTHER'S DAY FUN RHYME

Use large placards with the letters M-O-T-H-E-R and have members of your youth group present this fun rhyme for their mothers.

**M** is for my muddy feet
That tracked across the floor,
All the many, many times
I slammed the kitchen door.

Those days are gone forever,
My footprints you'll not see,
Especially if I'm slippin in
At twenty-five 'til three.

**O** is for orange juice and oatmeal,
I've spilled upon my clothes;
And aren't you glad, dear mother,
You no longer wipe my nose?

I'll clean my room, set the table,
My efforts'll deserve a star,
I'll even hang up all my clothes,
If you'll let me have the car.

There's lots of words that start with **T**,
About my childhood days,
Like Tinker-toys and tooting trains,
And temperatures and trays.

You need not worry and fret now
When I'm feeling not my best,
I'm really not so sick, you know,
I'm only facing tests.

**H** is for her loving heart,
And a hug and gentle hand
That shaped a lot of hamburgers
And dumped a lot of sand. . . .

From tennis shoes and pockets,
She combed it from my hair,
I'll need help again, I'm sure,
As long as the beach is there.

**(E)** Each day I'm grateful for her help
For everything she's done,
To help me shape up as I should
And be a perfect son.

I've given up lots of habits,
I'd rather not say which,
In case I try them just once more
Before I find my niche.

**(R)** "Really? Really? Really!"
Her frustration sometimes shows.
But she comes through, with colors true,
As everybody knows.

She puts up with lots of things,
I know that it's a chore,
I'll try not ask for favors,
If she'll drive me to school *once* more.

## PARENT BLUNDERS AND TEEN GOOFS

Here's a revealing questionnaire that would be effective on either Mother's Day or Father's Day. Give each kid a mimeographed sheet which contains two columns of numbered "Yes" and "No" answers, ten to each column. Then give the following questions to them orally and have them circle their response after each question. The kids should be as honest as they possibly can, and they need not put their names on their answer sheets.

In column one they must answer questions relating to their parents' attitudes toward them, and in column two, questions about their attitudes towards their parents. The total number of "yes" and "no" answers in each column can be totaled after the quiz and may then be used as a basis for discussion. Normally, whenever the parents score a high number of "no" answers, so do the kids (and vice versa). For example, if a kid says his parents do not act like they trust him, he will undoubtedly answer "no" to the questions about trying to earn and keep his parents' trust. The answers should show that both parents and teens have a fifty-fifty share of the responsibility for their problems.

*Parent Blunders:*

1. Do your parents listen to you when you have a family discussion?
2. Do your parents act like they trust you?
3. Do your parents treat your friends nicely and make them feel welcome?
4. Do your parents admit their mistakes when they have been wrong?
5. Do your parents openly express and show their affection for you?
6. Do your parents avoid comparing you to brothers or sisters, or other youth?
7. Do your parents keep the promises they make to you?
8. Do your parents show their appreciation and give you credit when you do something good?
9. Do your parents set a good example for you in their personal honesty?
10. Do your parents use the kind of language in front of you that they told you to use?

*Teen Goofs:*

1. Do you listen to your parents when they want to share an idea or advice with you?
2. When your parents say "NO" to your plans, do you accept that answer without complaining?
3. Do you try to understand the pressures and problems that sometimes make parents grumpy and hard to live with?
4. Do you say "Thank you" for everything that your parents do for you?
5. Do you try to plan something nice that you can do for your parents occasionally?
6. Do you say "I'm sorry" when you know you have been out of line or have said or done something you shouldn't?
7. Do you try to earn and keep your parents' trust by doing what they expect of you?
8. Do you play fair with them and discuss things honestly, without covering up for yourself?
9. Do you ask your parents' advice about decisions that you have to make?
10. Do you try to avoid problems and arguments by doing what you're supposed to before you have to be told?

## WHAT I WANT FOR MY CHILDREN

This could be a good discussion starter on Mother's Day or Father's Day. Have the kids in the group think of themselves as parents. They should imagine that they have a child and that it is now their job to be a really good parent to that child. Then have them answer questions like these:

1. What will be the best way for me to make sure that my child has a happy, fulfilling life?
2. What will be the best way for me to teach my children my values and beliefs?
3. How will I discipline my child?
4. What are some things that will be "no-no's," that is, things that I don't want them to do?

5. What are some things that I do want them to do?
6. What will we do as a family to have fun?
7. What do I hope that my child will think of me when he or she is grown?
8. What do I think my child's greatest problem will be, and how will I help him or her to overcome that problem?

# New Year's Day

## BIRTH OF A NEW YEAR PARTY

Since the new year is usually characterized by the exit of "Father Time" and the entrance of "Baby New Year," this is an event based on "babies." Everybody should come dressed like a baby, if possible, wearing diapers, "jammies," bibs, and the like. Then the following games can be played:

1. *Best Dressed Baby:* Judge for the best baby costume worn to the party.
2. *Baby Picture Guess:* Everyone should be told to bring a baby picture of himself, and you should hang them all up on the wall with a number beside each one. Then give everyone a piece of paper with the corresponding numbers on it, and he should try to match the pictures with the names of the people at the party. You can also have people vote for the "most beautiful baby," "ugliest baby," etc.
3. *Baby Burp:* This is a competition for couples. Boys are instructed to drink a bottle of soda pop while the girls slap them on the back. Do it one at a time, and judge for the loudest, longest "burp."
4. *Baby Buggy Race:* Get an old baby carriage or stroller for each team. Then have a race, relay style, with each person pushing the carriage around a goal and back with a teammate riding on it.
5. *Bottle Drinking Contest:* Give contestants a baby bottle full of warm milk. The first to finish it is the winner.
6. *Diaper Changing Contest:* Give the girls large diapers (ripped up sheets) and have them race to diaper the guys (over their pants, of course). Or, let the boys race to see who can change a diaper on a doll the fastest.
7. *Baby Food Race:* Pair off in couples. Have the girls feed a jar of baby food to the guys. The first to finish is the winner.
8. *Crying Contest:* See who can cry the loudest, most convincingly, and so on.

## NEW YEAR'S EVE EVE PARTY

With holiday driving becoming more and more dangerous on New Year's Eve, why not have a New Year's Eve Eve Party instead? Celebrate New Year's Eve Eve at midnight. The kids can have all the fun of New Year's Eve and then stay home to babysit on the real New Year's Eve.

## NEW YEAR'S RESOLUTIONS

First discuss the meaning of the words, "New Year's Resolution." Ask kids to share some resolutions that they have made in the past and what happened to them. Did they last? How long? Next, introduce the word "covenant" and ask the kids to compare that word with the word "resolution." What is the difference between the two? (One important difference is that a resolution is generally a private thing, and a covenant is a promise or agreement made publicly between two or more people.)

After some discussion, have the kids form small groups of three, preferably with friends that they know fairly well. Then give them ten minutes or so to write a few "New Year's Covenants." After they are completed, each person should then share his or her covenants with the other members of the small group and ask for feedback. Are they too vague? Impossible to keep? Too easy? Inappropriate? Each person is allowed to rewrite his or her covenants based on the feedback received. Finally, the kids can share their rewritten covenants and perhaps discuss practical ways they plan to put them into practice.

## RESOLUTION REVIEW

Have everyone in the group write down a few New Year's resolutions after a discussion on the meaning of commitments and promises. When all are finished, have them place their resolutions envelopes and seal them. They should also address the envelopes to themselves. The envelopes should be passed in, and the youth group leader should hang on to them for a few weeks (or months) and then mail them out to the kids. At that time, they will be reminded of their resolutions and will be able to see how well they are doing towards keeping them. This could be discussed at another meeting.

# St. Patrick's Day

## LIMERICK CONTEST

A limerick is a nonsense poem that is closely connected to Ireland, as the name comes from the city of Limerick on the banks of the river Shannon, in Ireland. Here's a sample:

> A girl that my grandmother knows,
> Had hair that reached down to her toes.
> It was beautiful to see,
> But unfortunately,
> It was all growing out of her nose.

The above example may not be a classic, but it gives you the idea. The first, second, and fifth lines rhyme, and the third and fourth lines rhyme.

Divide the group into "Irish Families" and see which family can come up with the best limerick within a given time limit. They can read them out loud, and a panel of judges can determine the "winner." It's a good exercise in creativity.

## SHAMROCK PUZZLES

Make some shamrocks out of green construction paper and then cut them up into pieces. You should cut each shamrock into the same number of pieces, but be sure you cut each shamrock differently. Each person should be given a piece of a shamrock, and the object will be to try and match her piece with others to get a complete, perfect-fitting shamrock. The first group to get their shamrock put together is the winner.

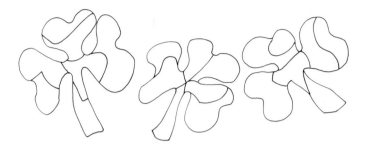

## SHAMROCK QUIZ

Give the group the following "clues," and see who can be first to come up with all the answers. Each answer is a word that can be made using the letters in the word "shamrock."

| Clues | Answers |
|---|---|
| 1—An Irish city | Cork |
| 2—A month of the year | March |
| 3—Member of the human body | Arm |
| 4—Article of man's apparel | Sock |
| 5—A common article of food | Ham |
| 6—A bright planet | Mars |
| 7—A detested pest | Roach |
| 8—Used in making towels | Crash |
| 9—Replaced by the auto | Hack |
| 10—An instrument of torture | Rack |
| 11—What we lack when the banks close | Cash |
| 12—Common means of transportation | Car |
| 13—An article used in disguise | Mask |
| 14—Swampy land | Marsh |
| 15—Something very solid | Rock |
| 16—Something not real | Sham |
| 17—A well-known uncle | Sam |
| 18—A gospel writer | Mark |
| 19—Noah's boat | Ark |
| 20—To mimic | Mock |

## ST. PATRICK'S DAY SCAVENGER HUNT

Here's a great scavenger-hunt list for St. Patrick's Day. Just divide up into groups of any number, give each group the list, and set a time limit. The group that can go out into the neighborhood and bring back the most green items is the winner.

1. Green Lettuce Leaf
2. Green Pear
3. Green Piece of Paper
4. Green Lima Bean
5. Green Stamps
6. Four Leaf Clover or Shamrock
7. Green Garter
8. One-Dollar Bill
9. Green Pencil
10. Green Turtle (Live)
11. Green Button
12. Green Tennis Shoe (Left Foot)
13. Green Hair Ribbon
14. Bottle of Jade East
15. Green Tooth Pick
16. Green Fingernail Polish
17. Green Bathing Suit
18. Green Tooth Brush
19. Green Palm Leaf
20. Green Hand Soap
21. Green Straw
22. Green Dixie Cup
23. Green Shoe Lace
24. Green Sweater
25. Green Sucker
26. Green Pickle
27. Green Sock
28. Avocado
29. 7-inch Green String
30. Green Ink
31. Green Balloon—Blown up
32. Green Newspaper
33. Green Flower
34. Green Fish
35. Green Key
36. Green Onion
37. Green Plastic Record
38. Green Book
39. One Pair Green Sunglasses
40. Green Frog (Live)
41. Green Petticoat
42. Green Lipstick
43. Green Lamp Shade
44. Green Ping-Pong Paddle
45. Green Gum
46. Green Ticket Stub
47. Green Postage Stamp (less than 18¢)
48. Jolly Green Giant Picture
49. Green Lime
50. Green Stuffed Animal

# Washington's Birthday

## CHERRY JUBILEE

Divide the kids into two groups of equal number and have them assemble in different corners of one end of the room. The leader of each group should be given three or four large cherries (either real or imitation). When the signal is given, one contestant from each group must place the cherries on the back of his left hand and race with them in this position to the goal at the other end of the room and back. If any of the cherries roll off, the runner must pick them up unassisted and continue. When the first player returns, the second player must go, and so on until all have had a try.

## CHOPPING DOWN THE CHERRY

Fill a bowl full of flour, pack it in real good, and then turn it over on a hard surface like a table-top. Remove the bowl, and if all goes well, you should have an upside-down bowl-shaped pile of flour. On top of that place one cherry. Have the group gather around and have each person, one at a time, take a knife and cut away part of the flour from around the cherry. A person can cut only one "slice," but it can be as large or as small as she chooses. The object is to not let the cherry fall from its perch. If it does, you lose. It's challenging and fun.

## CROSSING THE DELAWARE

Mark lines on the floor that represent a winding river about four feet wide using chalk or tape. Then have the group form a circle that crosses over the river in two places.

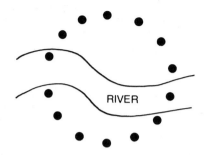

On go, the circle should start moving, and when the whistle is blown by the leader, the group must freeze. Whoever is caught "in the river" is out of the game. Jumping over the river is not allowed, nor is any hesitation before crossing the river. For more excitement, make the river wider. The leader should not be watching the group when he or she blows the whistle. Keep eliminating down to the last person, who is then declared the winner.

## I CANNOT TELL A LIE

This is a good game for smaller groups that works great for a Washington's Birthday celebration. Everyone should be seated in a circle. Each person should have a pencil and paper. They are asked to answer questions similar to, Where were you all day yesterday? with four answers. In other words, they must write down four places where they were yesterday. But one of them must be a lie, and the other three must be true.

After everyone is finished writing, go around the group and ask each person to read his four answers. The group must try to guess which one is the lie. If they are wrong, then that person gets a point. If they guess correctly, then no point is given. Do this with five or six different questions, and the person who gets the most points is given the distinction of being the best "liar" in the group.

# And Etcetera

## ALL-PURPOSE PARTY

There are several holidays that occur around the end of the year, and with an "all-purpose party" you can celebrate them all at the same time. You can call it a "Halloween-Thanksgiving-Christmas-New Year's Eve Party" if you prefer and divide the evening up into four segments. Each segment can be thirty to forty-five minutes of celebration of each of the four holidays. Begin with a Halloween party complete with costumes, Halloween games, cider and doughnuts, ghost stories, etc. Then move to another room which can be decorated for Thanksgiving and serve turkey with all the trimmings. Then move to a Christmas party with a gift exchange, a visit from Santa, Christmas carols, and so on. Wrap up the evening with a New Year's party and have the clocks appropriately set so that midnight comes when you want it. Have plenty of noisemakers, and sing a rousing chorus of "Auld Lang Syne." This will take care of all four holidays at once and can be done anytime in November or December.

## LITTLE-KNOWN HOLIDAYS

Here are some dates taken from *Chase's Calendar of Annual Events* (Apple Tree Press, Flint, Michigan) that can be used for unusual holiday celebrations. Sometimes it can really be fun to have a big party to celebrate "Buzzard Day" or "National Artichoke Week." You might even want to make up a special "holiday" of your very own.

| | |
|---|---|
| *JANUARY* | (Louisiana Yam Supper Season) |
| 2–8 | Save the Pun Week (have a Pun party) |
| 7 | Bulfinch Exchange Festival in Fukuoka, Japan |
| *FEBRUARY* | |
| 4–6 | Iceworm Festival in Cordova, Alaska |
| 6–9 | Annual Camel Wrestling Competition in Yenipazar, Turkey |
| 7–11 | National Pay Your Bills Week |
| *MARCH* | (International Hamburger-Pickle Month) |
| 1–5 | Return Your Borrowed Book Week |
| 6–11 | National Procrastination Week |
| 15 | Buzzard Day in Hinkley, Ohio |
| *APRIL* | (Anti-Noise Month) |
| 1–9 | Daffodil Festival in Puyallup, Washington |
| 3–9 | National Laugh Week (Would you believe silent laughter?) |
| 6–15 | National Artichoke Week |
| 22–26 | National Baby Week |
| 23–26 | Write a Poem Fortnight |
| *MAY* | (Car Care Month, International Play Your Own Harpsichord Month, and Senior Citizen's Month) |
| 18–27 | International Pickle Week (see March) |
| *JUNE* | (Cat and Kitten Month, Fight the Filthy Fly Month, and National Ragweed Control Month) |
| 4–10 | Girl-Watching Week (Try a mock beauty contest.) |
| 15 | Dragon Boat Festival in Hong Kong |
| 17 | National Hollering Contest in Dunn, North Carolina |
| 17–18 | Fudge-Off Finals in Mackinac Island, Michigan (dedicated to improving the art of making fudge) |
| 19–25 | National Fink Week (aimed at restoring the dignity "to the honorable surname of Fink") |
| 24 | National Rooster Crowing Contest in Grants Pass, Oregon |

| | |
|---|---|
| *JULY* | (National Hot Dog Month, National Barbecue Month, and Souvenir Month) |
| 2 | Stone Skipping and Ge-Plunking Open Tournament at Mackinac Island |
| 7–9 | Custer's Last Stand Reenactment at Hardin, Montana (to reenact the battle from the Indian point of view) |
| *AUGUST* | (Sandwich Month) |
| 1–6 | National Clown Week |
| 4 | Lizzie Bordon Liberation Day |
| 11–12 | Hobo convention in Britt, Iowa |

| | |
|---|---|
| 19 | National Chimneys Jousting Tournament at Mt. Solon, Virginia |
| 24 | National Hula Hoop Championships in Hollywood |
| *SEPTEMBER* | (American Youth Month) |
| 2 | Moustache Day |
| 6 | Be Late for Something Day, sponsored by the Procrastinator's Club of America |
| 24–30 | National Dog Week |
| *OCTOBER* | (Country Music Month, Gourmet Adventures Month, and Pizza Festival Time Month) |
| 2–8 | Newspaper Week |
| 5–14 | National Macaroni Week |
| 9–15 | International Letter Writing Week |
| 25–Nov. 2 | National Pretzel Week |
| 29–Nov. 4 | National Mushroom Week |
| *NOVEMBER* | (Think-of-What-You-Can-Replace-With-Plastic Month) |
| 5–11 | International Cat Week |
| 13–17 | National Split Pea Soup Week |
| 21–27 | Elderly Gentlemen Week |
| 23–Jan. 1 | National Indigestion Season (proclaimed by the baking soda people) |

| DECEMBER | (Model Railroad Month) |
|---|---|
| 2 | Whirling Dervish Festival in Konya, Turkey |
| 16 | Man Will Never Fly Memorial Day (celebrated by the Man Will Never Fly Society) |
| 21 | Forefather's Day (commemorating the Pilgrim's landing) |
| 31 | Day of the Namahage in Japan (Sluggards are given an opportunity to change their minds and go to work or be punished by devils.) |

## ONCE-A-YEAR BIRTHDAY PARTY

This idea is excellent for groups of all ages. Decorate a large room for a birthday party. Arrange twelve tables and decorate each according to the events of that particular month in the year, e.g., swimming in June, Halloween in October. Make a birthday cake for each month and set it at the appropriate table along with ice cream and party favors.

Invite each person in the group to sit at the table corresponding to his birthday month. The program could include awards recognizing the oldest person, the youngest, the person with a birthday on a holiday, etc. Also, you could play some games like these:

1. *Birthday Barnyard:* This one is best with big groups. Give each person a list like the one below. After all have received the list they are instructed to look at the action described for the month of their birthday. With the lights turned out, they are to immediately stand up and make the appropriate action. As soon as they find another person doing the same thing, they must lock arms and look for the rest of the team. As soon as all the team is together, they must sit down. The first team to find all its members wins.

> January—Shout "Happy New Year!"
> February—Say "Be My Valentine"
> March—Blow (wind)
> April—Hop (Easter Bunny)
> May—Say "Mother, May I?"
> June—Say "Will you marry me?"
> July—Make fireworks sounds
> August—Sing "Take me out to the ball game"
> September—Fall down (fall)
> October—Shout "Boo!"
> November—Say "Gobble-Gobble"
> December—Say "Ho Ho Ho, Merrry Christmas!"

2. *Happy Birthday Race:* Divide the group into teams. On a signal each team must line up according to their date of birth, with the youngest person on the end of the line and the oldest on the other. Any team out of order after the time limit (or the last team to get in the correct order) loses.

185

## PARTY-MAKING PARTY

This is a great idea for youth groups that want to have parties and want to help others. Have your youth group put on a party for those groups you want to help. You could have a Sweetheart's Banquet for an old folks home or the elderly in your congregation; an Easter Egg hunt for an orphanage or special education group; a Christmas party for underprivileged kids; or a Thanksgiving Banquet for underprivileged kids, widows, or college students who are away from home.